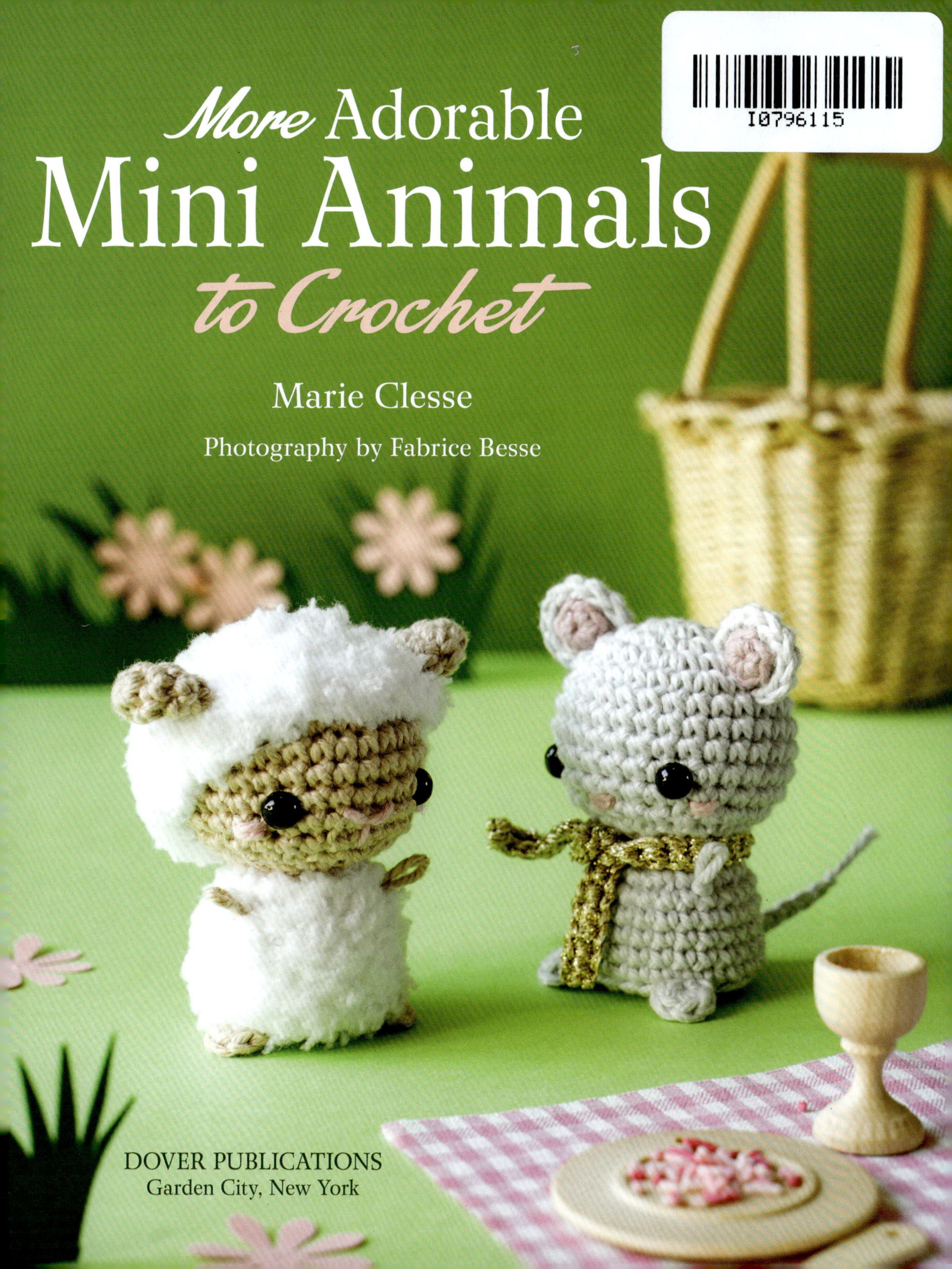

More Adorable Mini Animals *to Crochet*

Marie Clesse

Photography by Fabrice Besse

DOVER PUBLICATIONS
Garden City, New York

THE YARNS

The editor and the author thank DMC for the magnificent yarns
that were used for the creation of the designs.

This Dover edition, first published in 2025, is a new English translation of *Nouveaux adorables mini animaux* by
Marie Clesse, with photography by Fabrice Besse, published by Mango, Paris, France, in 2021.
The original French work has been translated into English by Janet Ross Snyder.

ISBN-13: 978-0-486-85485-4
ISBN-10: 0-486-85485-X

Publisher: Betina Cochran
Acquisitions Editor: Allyson D'Antonio
Managing Editorial Supervisor: Susan Rattiner
Cover Designer: Peter Donahue
Creative Manager: Marie Zaczkiewicz
Interior Designer: Jennifer Becker
Production: Pam Weston, Tammi McKenna, Ayse Yilmaz

Printed in China
85485X01 2025
www.doverpublications.com

Introduction

When I wrote the first volume of *Adorable Mini Animals to Crochet*, I felt a mixture of excitement and fear. Even though you loved seeing all these little animals appear on my social media pages, what if you didn't really enjoy crocheting them yourselves?

I was reassured very quickly! Your passion was immediately evident, so much so that the book had to be reprinted almost as soon as it came out. As a result, when the question of whether I would launch into a new book project arose, I didn't hesitate. We had to make choices about what to include in the first book, and I wanted to offer you all those designs that had been put aside.

So, in this book, you will find detailed instructions for making twenty new mini animals, grouped into five different worlds.

Some of them may be familiar to you because I have been crocheting them for a long time already. Others are totally new, and I hope you will like them just as much!

Now, if you liked the first *Adorable Mini Animals to Crochet*, I invite you to take another dive into this delightful world and expand your collection.

1, 2, 3 . . . start crocheting!

Marie

Contents

Animals of the Savanna

pp. 32–39

Leopard and Zebra

pp. 32 and 34

Ostrich

p. 36

Giraffe

p. 38

Forest Animals

Peacock and Frog, pp. 40 and 42

Panda and Monkey

pp. 43 and 44

Farm Animals

Hen and Chick, pp. 46 and 48

Lamb and Mouse

pp. 49 and 50

The Wee World

Bee, p. 52

Ladybug

p. 53

Snail

p. 54

Butterfly

p. 56

Sea Creatures

Ray, p. 58

Baby Seal

p. 59

Crab

p. 61

Blue Tang

p. 62

Materials

YARNS

The designs in this book have been crocheted with DMC Happy Cotton yarn, which I find perfect for *amigurumi*. You can easily find this yarn in stores and online shops.
For each design, you will find the yarn and thread colors used and the necessary quantities of each. However, feel free to use the yarn of your choice. If you choose another yarn, you must make sure to use a smaller crochet hook than the one recommended on the yarn ball. That way you can avoid having holes between the stitches and won't see the stuffing through the holes.
If you are a beginner, make sure to choose a yarn that is tightly spun. A yarn that splits can become very frustrating for a beginner (or even for a seasoned crocheter). In general, you are better off working with good quality yarns. They make the work much more pleasant.
Do not hesitate to try some of these patterns with a thicker cotton yarn, like DMC Natura Just Cotton Medium, to be crocheted with a 3mm or 3.5mm hook, according to the suppleness desired. That will give you even larger animals that are 3⅛in (8cm) high instead of 2⅜in (6cm), perfect for making little stuffed toys or cute decorations for a child's room.

HOOKS

This table shows the correspondence between metric crochet hook sizes, US sizes, and UK sizes.

Metric	US	US Steel	UK	UK Steel
2mm	0	4	14	2½
2.25mm	B-1	2	13	1½
2.5mm	B-1 or C-2	2 or 1	13 or 12	1½ or 1
4mm	G-6		8	

To crochet these miniatures, I use a 2.25mm crochet hook and crochet tightly, to make the figures quite rigid. However, you can choose to crochet them with a 2.5mm crochet hook to produce a result that is a little more supple. Your animals will then be a little bigger as well. I also use a 2.5mm crochet hook for some parts crocheted in plush yarn. Nevertheless, I advise against using a larger crochet hook with this thickness of cotton because the stitches would then be much more spaced out, and that would be very noticeable on such small designs.
I cannot stress enough how important it is to invest in a good quality crochet hook. For my part, I prefer ergonomic crochet hooks, even though I hold my crochet hook in a nonstandard way, like a knife. But others may prefer a simple steel or aluminum hook. Do not hesitate to test a crochet hook design before launching into the purchase of a complete set. A good crochet hook should slide easily between the stitches, and its point must not get caught on the threads, to avoid splitting them.

STUFFING

I use polyester stuffing, treated for dust mites. It is easy to buy online, in 300g (10oz), 500g (1lb), or 1kg (2lb) bags. You can also find it in yarn shops, craft stores, or fabric stores, or in a pinch, you can reuse the stuffing from a pillow! It is difficult to indicate the quantity you will need for each design, because it all depends on whether you prefer to stuff lightly or firmly. However, a 300g (10oz) bag will likely be enough to make all the designs in this book.

To make some of these mini animals, I also use plastic pellets, about 5mm in diameter. These little granules make it possible to give a certain weight to the body and thus a better balance to the little figures. They are a good alternative to classic stuffing, because they do not cause the body to bulge, and they make it possible for the base to remain flat.

If you don't want to use plastic pellets, I would advise you to use a stuffing that is not too fluffy, to avoid deforming the body and to keep its base nice and flat.

If you use plastic pellets, it is important to use a small crochet hook so that the stitches are quite tight and the little pellets cannot escape.

The stuffing (polyester batting or pellets) must be dense enough to give shape to the project, but not so dense that it spreads out the stitches; if you stuff too densely, you will see the stuffing between each stitch, which is not pleasing and might even prove dangerous for young children.

Tip: I always wait several hours after having stuffed the head before sewing it onto the body. It is then easier to judge whether a little stuffing is missing somewhere, and to make adjustments so that the head is nicely round and harmonious.

SAFETY EYES

The size to be used is indicated for each design (between 4.5mm and 8mm [1/5in and 1/3in]). These plastic eyes are sold with a washer that attaches to the back on a notched stem; this guarantees that the eyes cannot be removed. They are rather difficult to find in small sizes. If you do not find them at your favorite local shop, I suggest that you look for them on the internet, where you will find a vast selection. You may also use black beads instead, or even embroider the eyes with black thread, which is recommended if your *amigurumi* are likely to be handled by children younger than three years of age.

OTHER MATERIALS

- Embroidery thread. I use DMC Pearl Cotton size 5.
- Plush yarn. I use Baby Smiles Lenja Soft, by Schachenmayr.
- Yarn needle and a finer needle for the Pearl Cotton threads.
- Pins to hold the pieces together while assembling them.
- Stitch markers. If you have none, you may instead use a small safety pin, a paper clip, or a small piece of thread passed through the stitch to mark it.
- Scissors.
- Flat pliers. They are very useful for stuffing the small crocheted parts, for adding a bit of stuffing to a precise location, or for pulling a needle through several thicknesses of wool and stuffing (and for saving your fingers).
- Optional: pipe cleaners (chenille stems) for the tails of certain animals, and a permanent felt marker to color the cheeks.

Techniques

The following explanations are given for someone who holds the crochet hook in the right hand. If you are left-handed, you will need to follow the explanations using a mirror image.

THE BASIC STITCHES

Chain stitch (ch): stitches in the air

1. Make a slip knot: insert the crochet hook in the loop of the knot, then using the point of the hook, catch the yarn coming from the ball or skein and bring it back through the loop. This slip knot is the starting point, but it never counts as a stitch.

2. To make a chain stitch (ch), yarn over (pass the yarn from back to front, over the crochet hook) and bring this yarn through the loop of the hook.

3. Repeat the second step until you obtain the desired number of stitches. The loop on the crochet hook must never be counted.

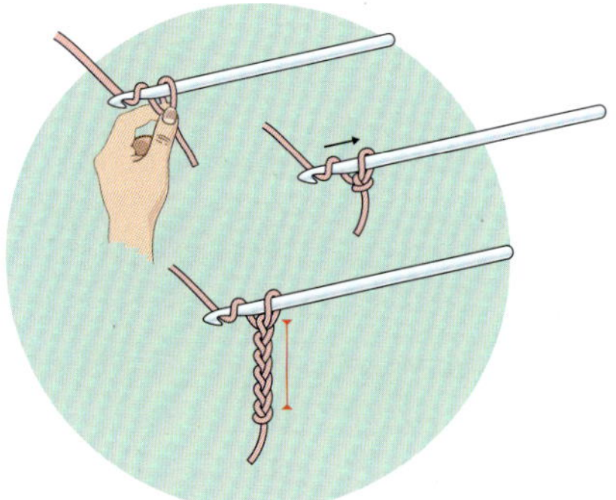

Slip stitch (sl st)

1. Insert the crochet hook in the stitch indicated.

2. Yarn over (yo) and bring the yarn through the stitch where the hook is and through the loop on the crochet hook. There should be one loop left on the crochet hook.

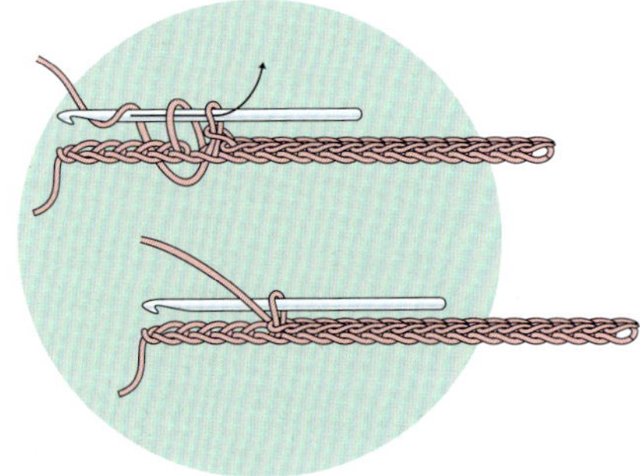

Single crochet (sc)

1. Insert the crochet hook into the stitch indicated.

2. Yarn over and bring the yarn through the stitch where your hook is. There should be two loops left on the hook.

3. Yarn over a second time and bring the yarn through the two loops. There should be one loop left on the crochet hook.

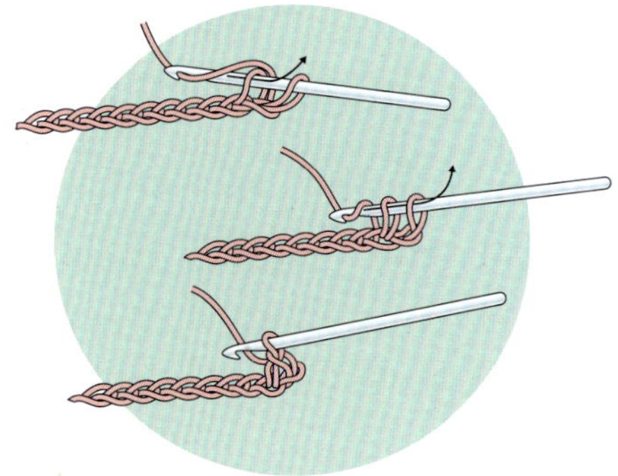

Half double crochet (hdc)

1. Yarn over, then insert the crochet hook into the stitch indicated.

2. Yarn over a second time and bring the yarn through the stitch where your hook is. There should be three loops on the crochet hook.

3. Yarn over one last time and bring the yarn through the three loops. There should be one loop left on the crochet hook.

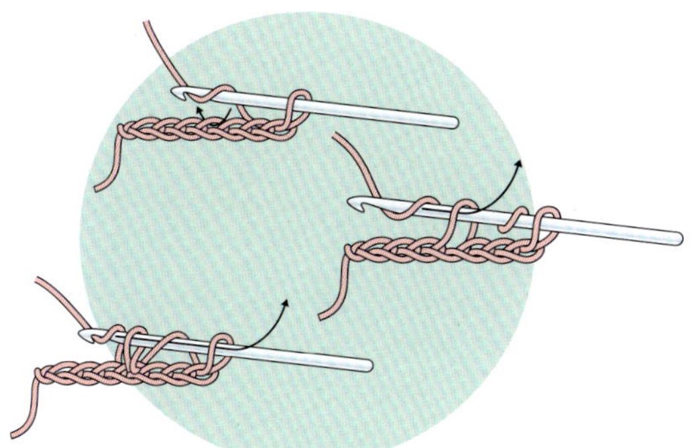

Double crochet (dc)

1. Yarn over, then insert the crochet hook into the stitch indicated.

2. Yarn over a second time and bring the yarn back through one loop. There should be three loops left on the crochet hook.

3. Yarn over a third time and bring the yarn back through two loops. There should be two loops on the crochet hook.

4. Yarn over one last time and bring the yarn back through the two loops. There should be one loop left on the crochet hook.

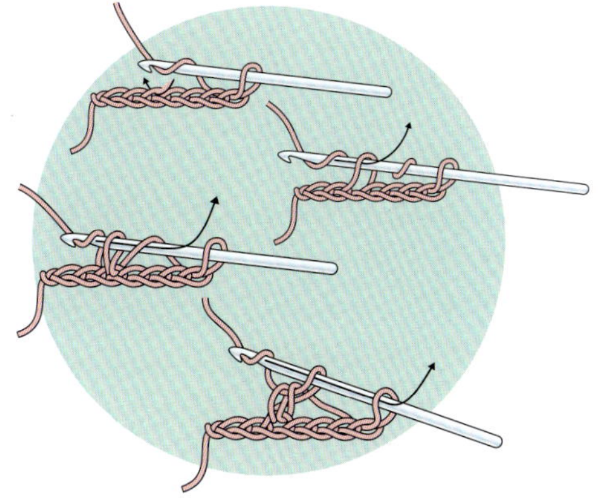

Treble crochet (tr)

1. Yarn over twice, then insert the crochet hook into the stitch indicated.

2. Yarn over a third time and bring the yarn back through the stitch where the crochet hook is. There should be four loops on the crochet hook.

3. Yarn over a fourth time and bring the yarn back through two loops. There should be three loops on the crochet hook.

4. Yarn over a fifth time and bring the yarn back through two loops. There should be two loops left on the crochet hook.

5. Yarn over one last time and bring the yarn back through the two loops. There should be one loop on the crochet hook.

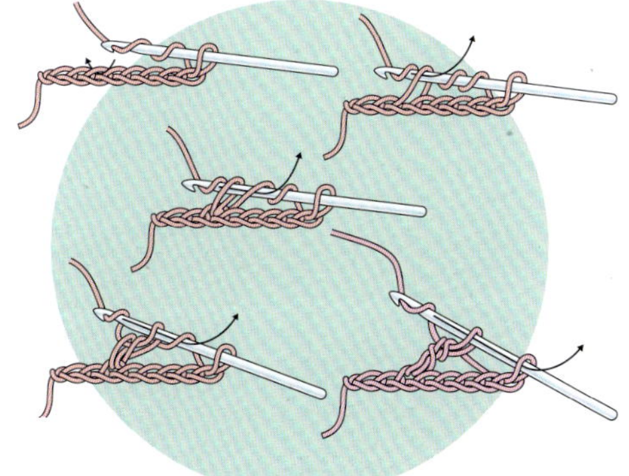

WHERE DO I INSERT THE CROCHET HOOK?

Unless otherwise indicated, always insert the hook from the front to the back.

In a chain

Insert the crochet hook into the upper loops of the chain. At the end of the chain, turn the work to the other side if you are crocheting in rows, or continue crocheting around the end of the chain to form an oval. In this case, continue crocheting on the chain, but this time in the lower loops.

In the stitches of a preceding row

The top of a crocheted stitch always has two small loops forming a horizontal V, no matter what type of stitch you are making. Unless you are instructed otherwise, always insert the crochet hook under both of these loops.

In the front loop only (FLO)

When this instruction is given, insert the crochet hook only in the front loop; that is, the loop of the V that is closest to you, on the front side of the work.

In the back loop only (BLO)

When this instruction is given, insert the crochet hook only in the back loop, that is, the loop of the V that is farthest away from you, on the back side of the work.

CROCHETING IN ROWS

Working in rows always starts with a chain that serves as a base. Crochet from right to left, turning the work (clockwise) at the end of each row. The last stitch crocheted thus becomes the first stitch of the next row. Working in rows makes it necessary to start with one or more chain stitches at the start of each row, depending on the height of the stitches that make up the row. (This will be indicated in the instructions for the designs concerned.)

CROCHETING IN THE ROUND

Working in the round (rnd) is the technique that is most often used to make *amigurumi*. It makes it possible to work continuously, without turning the work. Working in the round starts by making a magic circle (or a chain if you want to make an oval piece), and then you can work in a spiral, or you can close each round with a slip stitch.

Magic circle

This technique makes it possible to tighten the first round so that there is no hole at the center of the work. Hold the end of the yarn between the thumb and index finger of your left hand. Wrap it around your index finger, making one turn. Hold the part of the yarn connected to the ball with the middle finger and the ring finger. Insert the crochet hook under the loop formed on the index finger (between the yarn and the underside of your finger) and bring back the yarn attached to the ball. Make a chain stitch. The center ring is ready. Starting from there, crochet the number of stitches indicated in the loop thus formed. All that is left to do is to pull the end of the yarn to tighten the circle. Secure this yarn, if necessary, by crocheting it into the stitches of the second round.

Crocheting in a spiral

This technique consists of crocheting continuously, without closing the rounds.
At the end of a round, simply continue crocheting in the next stitch, which is the first stitch of the round that you just finished.
It is important to use a stitch marker to keep your place in your work. Place this marker on the first stitch of each round. On the last stitch of the round, remove the marker, make the first stitch of the following round, and place the marker over it.

Crocheting in closed rounds

This technique consists of closing each round before moving on to the following one.
After having made the last stitch of the round, make a slip stitch in the first stitch made at the start of the round. This stitch closes the round, and it is never counted in the count of stitches of the round.
To start a new round, first make the number of chain stitches to reach the correct height corresponding to the type of stitch that you are going to crochet on this round: one chain for single crochet, two for half-double crochet, three for double crochet, etc. When you work in closed rounds, this chain is not counted in the stitch count for the round. Next, make the first stitch of the new round in the first stitch of the preceding round (the same one in which you just made a slip stitch).
Even though it is easier to keep your place in the work by crocheting in this manner, I advise you to mark the first stitch of each round all the same.
I am often asked why I crochet certain parts in closed rounds in the designs. It is, in fact, more common to crochet amigurumi in a spiral. Crocheting in closed rounds has its advantages. First of all, it makes color changes clearer for a striped design. For certain pieces, it also makes it possible to have a result that is straighter or more level. However, if you are having difficulty with this technique, it is quite possible to crochet in a spiral instead.

Trick: It is easy to make the demarcation that is formed with the slip stitch that closes each round almost invisible. All you have to do is tighten this stitch to the maximum while crocheting the rest normally!

INCREASES

An increase consists of simply making two stitches in the same stitch of the preceding round or row. The *amigurumi* or other crocheted objects are made essentially with single crochet. Also, when you see the abbreviation "inc," it means that you must make two single crochets in the same stitch.

Sometimes you must increase another type of stitch. In this case, the instruction will be, for example, "two half double crochets in the same stitch." You may also be instructed to make "three single crochets in the same stitch." Follow the instructions exactly to obtain the expected results.

DECREASES

A decrease consists of crocheting two stitches together to obtain only one at that place. I mainly use the technique of invisible decreases. When you find the abbreviation "dec," it means that you must crochet two single crochets together. To do that, instead of inserting the crochet hook under both loops of the stitch, insert it in the front loop of the stitch, then immediately insert it in the front loop of the following stitch. Next make a single crochet. If you must make a decrease in a half double, follow the same method: yarn over as you would do for a normal half double, then insert the crochet hook in the front loop of the first stitch and immediately afterward in the front loop of the following stitch. Yarn over again, and bring the yarn back through these two front loops. Then yarn over again and bring the yarn back through the three loops on the crochet hook.

To decrease the number of stitches of a round, it is sometimes necessary to flow the stitches together. This consists of making incomplete stitches (you do not make the last yarn over of these stitches), in order to flow them together when you make the final, common yarn over. For example, to flow two single stitches together, you must follow these steps:

- Insert the crochet hook as indicated in the following stitch, yarn over and bring back the yarn. At this point, there are two loops on the crochet hook.
- Instead of finishing this single stitch, insert the crochet hook in the following stitch, yarn over, and bring back the yarn. There are now three loops on the crochet hook.
- Do a last yarn over and bring back the yarn through the three loops on the crochet hook. Now there is only one loop on the hook. To flow together another type of stitch, always proceed in the same manner by following all the steps of the stitch in question, except for the last yarn over. After having made the number of incomplete stitches to flow together (there can be more than two of them), do a last yarn over and bring back the yarn through all the loops on the crochet hook.

COLOR CHANGES

It is important to do a color change at the place indicated in order to obtain the desired result. But, to obtain a neat result, you must start at the previous stitch!

To do this, when you crochet the last stitch before the color change, follow these steps:

- Start the single crochet normally. Insert the crochet hook, yarn over, and pull the yarn toward the stitch. You now have two loops on the crochet hook.
- Change the color at that moment by doing a yarn over with the new color, and bring this yarn through the two loops on the hook. There is now one loop of the new color on the crochet hook.

Next, continue to crochet with this new color. Make a knot on the back side of the work with the yarn of the old color and the starting yarn of the new color.

Sometimes you have to make repeated color changes. In this case, it is preferable not to cut the old color yarn, but to keep it attached so that you can start to crochet with it again a few stitches later or in the next round.

RIGHT SIDE OR WRONG SIDE OF THE STITCHES?

It is sometimes difficult for beginners to figure out which is the right side or the wrong side of their work.

If you are right-handed, when you insert the crochet hook from the front to the back (that is, from the outside to the inside as the piece begins to take its rounded shape), the right side of the work is toward you (that is, the outside as the piece begins to take shape).
For pieces crocheted in the round, it is easier to crochet if you keep the right side of the work to the outside. You can choose to keep the back side visible for aesthetic reasons, but that presents two difficulties. First, the back side of the work is more disorganized. The back side of the single stitches presents a succession of little horizontal features that form lines, and the stitches are more difficult to see and to count. The right side of the single stitches forms little Vs that are much easier to count. The major difficulty of the back side of the work is that it is more difficult to make invisible decreases there. Depending on the project that you are making, the decreases will be much more visible, and the finished product will be less attractive.
Train yourself to tell the front from the back with a few rounds of single crochet, and then observe the difference by testing other types of stitches!

FINISHING TECHNIQUES

Clean finishes are very important for an attractive result. Here is how to stop and close the various crocheted pieces

Stopping the yarn invisibly

When you work in a spiral, without closing the rounds, you obtain a sort of stairstep—the edge is not clean. To improve this uneven edge, the instructions will ask you to finish with a slip stitch.
Cut the yarn to about 6in (15cm) and thread a needle with it. Skip over the following stitch and pass the needle under the next two back loops, going from the inside to the outside of the piece. Then pass the needle under the back loop of the slip stitch, by inserting it toward the inside of the piece. Make a knot on the back side of the work, or keep the length of the yarn for sewing, according to the instructions given.
This technique reproduces the two loops of a stitch above the stitch that you skipped. That makes it possible to obtain a clean result without having to change the number of stitches.

Closing a piece

After making the last stitch, cut the yarn off at a length of about 8in (20cm). With a needle, pass the yarn under the front loop of the following stitch, from the inside toward the outside. Do the same with all the stitches of the last crocheted round (generally 5 or 6 stitches). Then pull the yarn to close the opening.
Pass this yarn through the central hole and bring it out the other side of the crocheted piece. Adjust the tension so that it is well closed, but not enough to crush the piece. Pass the yarn through the piece once or twice more to secure the closure. Cut the yarn off flush with the surface of the piece.

ASSEMBLY

Sewing two open pieces together, edge to edge (head to body, for example)

When the last rounds of the two pieces have the same number of stitches, simply pass the thread alternately through one stitch of the body (from the inside to the outside) and then through a stitch of the head (from the outside to the inside). Make sure to verify the alignment of the head and the body after several sewing stitches, and restart if necessary by shifting the first stitch. After making the last stitch, make several more stitches to secure the closure, and then cut the thread off flush with the surface of the piece.

Sewing one piece onto another

These seams are a little more complicated and are often the pet peeve of crocheters! You will improve with practice. Position the piece to be sewn at the desired place, and pin it there so that it does not move. You must sew all the stitches of the last round to obtain a good-looking finish. Insert the needle under a thread of the closed piece, and then under both loops of the stitch of the last round, from the inside to the outside. Repeat this operation to sew all the stitches. Before making the last sewing stitches, add a little stuffing, if necessary. To finish, make several more stitches and cut the yarn off flush with the surface.

When crocheting these mini animals, you will notice that I sew certain elements before stuffing the head or the body. In fact, I often prefer to knot the sewing yarn on the inside, rather than stopping it by making several more stitches. Since the seams are small, like the animals, that ensures a more secure attachment.

For example, it will be difficult to have the front or back paws very tightly attached to the body without making a very tight knot on the back side of the work. On the other hand, the pellet stuffing used for the body does not help hold seams the way the polyester stuffing does (the stuffing used for the head), because the yarn does not get trapped on the inside by the pellets the way it does with the polyester stuffing. However, it is quite possible to sew all the elements of the head after having stuffed it, if you are more comfortable doing it that way.

For the body, if you find it difficult to figure out the position of the tummy or the tail, try this: lightly stuff the body with the polyester stuffing to give its shape; sew the necessary elements in place, being careful not to catch too much stuffing in the stitches; remove the extra stuffing (some will remain stuck to the sewing stitches, but this is not a problem); knot the yarn on the inside of the body; and finally, stuff the body with the plastic pellets.

EMBROIDERY

Several designs have instructions to embroider elements on the face (smile, eyebrows, etc.) If you know exactly where to place them, you can embroider before stuffing the piece and simply make a knot on the back side of the work. However, it is often difficult to evaluate the correct placement before stuffing. To embroider the elements after stuffing, take a long, fine needle and insert it between two stitches at the back of the piece, or in the stuffing through the opening of the piece, and bring it back out at the place where the embroidery should go. Embroider the elements, then bring the thread back out exactly where it went in at the back of the piece, or through the stuffing again. Make a knot with the two threads, then push the knot inside the piece to make it invisible. With a needle, if necessary, push the two ends inside and cut off any part that is still sticking out.

SOME ADVICE BEFORE STARTING

To produce smooth work, do not tighten the stitches too much. The crochet hook should be able to pass easily through the stitches, and you should always keep the same tension on your yarn. If you are a beginner, practice making the basic stitches before starting the first design. That will help you feel at ease with the various basic stitches and their abbreviations, and not be obliged to constantly refer to the *Techniques* section of the book.

Feel free to vary the size of the crochet hook depending on the way you crochet: If you crochet more loosely, you may benefit from using a smaller crochet hook. On the other hand, if you tend to crochet more tightly, you may want to choose a larger crochet hook.

Read the instructions for a design completely before beginning to make sure that you understand everything and that you have not overlooked important information.

The estimated time to make each animal has been provided as a rough guide but may vary according to your crocheting experience. The duration indicated includes the time I spend reading the instructions as I go and crocheting at a relaxed speed.

Caution! These mini animals are not appropriate for children younger than three years old. However, if you decide to make a design for very young children, I advise you to replace the safety eyes with embroidered eyes, and to use a small crochet hook, to prevent holes between the stitches that could allow stuffing to come out.

ABBREVIATIONS

BL/BLO = back loop / back loop only
ch = chain stitch(es)
dc = double crochet(s)
dec = invisible decrease
FL/FLO = front loop / front loop only
hdc = half double crochet(s)
inc = increase
rnd(s) = round(s)
row(s) = row(s)
sc = single crochet(s)
st = stitch(es)
sl st = slip stitch(es)
tr = treble crochet(s)
( ) x 6 = crochet items in the parentheses six times
(6 st) = number of stitches for each round

Basic Shapes

HEAD

Embroidered eyes: To replace the safety eyes with embroidered eyes, embroider two or three small vertical black lines, one row high, starting from the location indicated for each eye.
Cheeks: I use two techniques for these mini animals. Some cheeks have been drawn on using a pink permanent felt marker with a diagonal point. Other cheeks have been embroidered by making a small line with two strands of yarn or thread at the bottom outside corner of each eye. The material necessary to draw or embroider the cheeks (felt marker or 10in [25cm] of pink thread) is not indicated at the start of each design. It is up to you to decide whether or not to make these cheeks.

Head A

Crochet in a spiral.
Rnd 1: 6 sc in a magic circle (6 st).
Rnd 2: 6 inc (12 st).
Rnd 3: (1 sc, 1 inc) x 6 (18 st).
Rnd 4: (1 sc, 1 inc, 1 sc) x 6 (24 st).
Rnd 5: (7 sc, 1 inc) x 3 (27 st).
Rnd 6: (3 sc, 1 inc, 5 sc) x 3 (30 st).
Rnds 7 to 10: 30 sc (30 st).
Rnd 11: (3 sc, 1 dec) x 6 (24 st).
For the **bee, lamb, ladybug, peacock, butterfly, hen, chick, mouse**: Insert the safety eyes between rnds 9 and 10, in st 12 and 19 of rnd 9.
For the **panda**: Insert the safety eyes between rnds 8 and 9, in st 12 and 19 of rnd 8.
Sew the ears and/or other elements of the head as indicated for each animal.
Start to stuff the head.
Rnd 12: (1 sc, 1 dec, 1 sc) x 6 (18 st).
Rnd 13: (1 dec, 1 sc) x 5, 1 dec, 1 sl st (12 st).
Cut the yarn to a length of 12in (30cm).
Finish stuffing the head. Sew the last elements and/or embroider the nose, the beak, or the mouth as indicated for each animal.

Head B

Crochet in a spiral.
Rnd 1: 6 sc in a magic circle (6 st).
Rnd 2: 6 inc (12 st).
Rnd 3: (1 sc, 1 inc) x 6 (18 st).
Rnd 4: (4 sc, 1 inc, 1 sc) x 3 (21 st).
Rnd 5: (1 sc, 1 inc, 5 sc) x 3 (24 st).
Rnd 6: (7 sc, 1 inc) x 3 (27 st).
Rnd 7: (3 sc, 1 inc, 5 sc) x 3 (30 st).
Rnds 8 to 10: 30 sc (30 st).
Then continue the instructions for Head A, starting from rnd 11.

BODY

Front legs

For the **bee, lamb, ladybug, frog, leopard, panda, monkey, mouse, zebra:**
Cut a piece of yarn to a length of 8in (20cm). Fold this yarn in half and make an overhand knot so as to obtain a small loop in the middle of the yarn, about 1/5in (5mm) in length.

Back legs

Design A: For the **lamb, ladybug, frog, leopard, panda, hen, chick, monkey, mouse, zebra**: Crochet 5 sc in a magic circle, keeping 4in (10cm) of yarn at the start and 6in (15cm) at the end.

Design B: For the **bee, peacock, butterfly**: Make the two legs by following the instructions for the front legs.

Body

Crochet in the round, in closed rnds. The sl st that closes each rnd and the ch that starts each rnd are not indicated in the instructions for better readability, but you must make them for each rnd. For more instructions, see the *Techniques* chapter, p. 24.

Rnd 1: 6 sc in a magic circle (6 st).
Rnd 2: 6 inc (12 st).
Rnd 3: (1 sc, 1 inc) x 6 (18 st).
Rnd 4: (1 sc, 1 inc, 1 sc) x 6 (24 st).
Rnd 5: 24 st in the BLO (24 st).
Rnds 6 to 9: 24 sc (24 st).

Design A: Attach the back legs to the body as follows: Using a needle, with the yarn left at the end, sew the 1st and last sc of the 1st leg in st 8 and 10 of rnd 5 (between rnds 4 and 5), and tie the starting and ending yarns of the leg in a knot several times on the inside of the body, tightening the knots well. Sew the second leg at the level of st 15 and 17 of rnd 5.

Design B: Attach the back legs to the body as follows: Using a needle, thread the 2 yarns of the 1st leg through st 9 and 10 of rnd 5 (between rnds 4 and 5) and knot them several times on the inside of the body, tightening the knots well. Thread the yarns of the 2nd leg through st 15 and 16 of rnd 5.

Rnd 10: (1 sc, 1 dec, 1 sc) x 6 (18 st).
Rnd 11: (1 sc, 1 dec) x 6 (12 st).

Cut the yarn to a length of 4in (10cm). Do not close the body yet.

Continue by following the instructions for Assembly.

ASSEMBLY

For the **bee, lamb, ladybug, frog, leopard, panda, peacock, butterfly, hen, chick, monkey, mouse**: Mark the 3rd st of rnd 11 of the body.

For the **zebra**: Mark the 2nd st of rnd 11 of the body.

Attach the front legs to the body for the animal concerned. Using a needle, thread both yarns of the 1st leg through st 8 and 9 of rnd 9 (between rnds 9 and 10), and knot them several times on the inside of the body, tightening the knots well. Thread the yarns of the 2nd leg through st 17 and 18 of rnd 9.

Sew the other elements of the body (tail, wings, etc.) according to the instructions given for each animal.

Close the body by stopping the yarn invisibly. Tie the yarn in a knot on the inside and cut it off.

Stuff the body using plastic pellets. The idea is to stuff sufficiently so that the body does not sag. However, you must not overstuff it; otherwise, the form of the body will be slightly stretched and the base will no longer be flat.

Sew the head to the body, using the yarn that you kept at the end of the head. Start by inserting the needle in the st marked on the last rnd of the body, from the inside to the outside. Next, insert the needle in the preceding st of the head (next-to-last st of rnd 13), from the outside to the inside. Sew all around, repeating these two steps.

Before making the last st, adjust some stuffing pellets, if necessary. Once the last st has been made, insert the needle in the neck and bring it out on the opposite side, also at the level of the neck. Then insert the needle just to one side and bring it out at the level of the neck again. Then insert the needle just to one side and bring it out at the level of the magic circle of the body. Insert the needle just beside the magic circle and bring it out at the level of the neck again. Take the time to give a good shape to the body and to adjust the tension of the yarn: this yarn must maintain the flat base of the body and keep it from becoming rounded, but without pulling it toward the center so much that it creates a hollow space. To finish, make some more st in the head to secure the yarn, and cut off the yarn flush with the surface.

Zebra

 2 hours 45 minutes

 pp. 6–7

Dimensions
Approximate height: 2¾in (7cm)

Preliminary information
The head and the body are crocheted in the round, in closed rounds. The sl st that closes each rnd and the ch that starts each rnd are not indicated in the instructions, for better readability, **but you must make them for each rnd**. For more instructions, see the *Techniques* chapter, p. 24. The color changes indicated at the end of a rnd for the head and the body should be made when making the **last sc** of the rnd, which means that the sl st that ends the rnd and the ch that start the next rnd will be made in the new color. This makes it possible to have invisible color changes.

Materials
› One 2.25mm crochet hook
› DMC Happy Cotton (¾oz–47yd [20g–43m]), shade 775, black, ¼oz (7g); shade 762, white, ¼oz (7g); shade 764, pale pink, 2¼yd (2m)
› Two 6mm (¼in) safety eyes

EARS x 2

In white. Crochet in a spiral.
Rnd 1: 4 sc in a magic circle (4 st).
Rnd 2: (1 inc, 1 sc) x 2 (6 st).
Rnd 3: (2 sc, 1 inc) x 2 (8 st).
Rnd 4: (1 dec, 1 sc) x 2, 1 dec (5 st).
Rnd 5: 1 sl st. Do not crochet the other st (5 st).
Cut the yarn to a length of 8in (20cm). Flatten the ear so as to have the yarn at one end.
With the pink yarn, embroider two small vertical lines, 2 rnds in height, in the middle of each ear. I prefer to embroider them beside the 2nd and 3rd st of rnd 4 so that the ear will be sewn in the right orientation. Tie the yarns, cut them off, and bring them back inside the ear.

MUZZLE

In pink. Crochet in a spiral.
Rnd 1: 5 sc in a magic circle (5 st).
Rnd 2: 5 inc (10 st).
Rnd 3: 9 sc, 1 sl st (10 st).
Cut the yarn to a length of 10in (25cm).

MANE

In black.
Ch 15, keeping 4in (10cm) of yarn before the slip knot; 1 sc in the 2nd st away from the crochet hook, 1 hdc in the same st; (2 hdc in the following st) x 12; 1 hdc, 1 sc, and 1 sl st in the following st.
Cut the yarn to a length of 12in (30cm).

HEAD

In black. Crochet in the round, in closed rnds.
Rnd 1: 6 sc in a magic circle (6 st).
In white.
Rnd 2: 6 inc (12 st).
In black.
Rnd 3: (1 sc, 1 inc) x 6 (18 st).
In white.
Rnd 4: (1 sc, 1 inc, 1 sc) x 6 (24 st).
In black.
Rnd 5: (7 sc, 1 inc) x 3 (27 st).
In white.
Rnd 6: (3 sc, 1 inc, 5 sc) x 3 (30 st).

In black.
Rnd 7: 30 sc (30 st).
In white.
Rnds 8 and 9: 30 sc (30 st).
In black.
Rnd 10: 30 sc (30 st).
In white.
Rnd 11: (3 sc, 1 dec) x 6 (24 st).
Insert the safety eyes between rnds 9 and 10, in st 12 and 19 of rnd 9.
Sew the ears on each side of the head, straddling rnds 4 to 6. Tie the yarns in a knot on the inside of the head and cut them off.
Start stuffing the head.
In black.
Rnd 12: (1 sc, 1 dec, 1 sc) x 6 (18 st).
In white.
Rnd 13: (1 dec, 1 sc) x 5, 1 dec, 1 sl st (12 st).
Cut the yarn to a length of 12in (30cm).
Finish stuffing the head.
Sew the muzzle between the eyes, straddling rnds 9 to 11 of the head.
With black yarn, embroider two little black dots on the muzzle to represent the nostrils.
Sew the mane with the yarn kept at the end.
Insert the needle in the back of the head, between rnds 11 and 12. Bring the needle out 1 rnd higher, and insert the yarn in the ch of the starting ch in which you made the 2 next-to-the-last hdc.
Insert the needle in the same place in the head and bring it out again 1 rnd higher. Thread the needle through the next ch and insert it in the same spot on the head. Continue like that 9 more times in a vertical line until you reach the magic circle of the head.
Sew the last 2 ch of the starting ch in the same way, in the direction of the muzzle. Bring the yarn inside the head and bring it out again through the stuffing, and do the same with the starting yarn. Tie the two together, cut off the excess yarn, and pull the yarn back into the stuffing.

TAIL

Crochet 2 yarns simultaneously: 1 black and 1 white. Ch 2, keeping 6/10in (1.5cm) of yarn before the slip knot. Tighten the starting knot well.
Cut the yarns to a length of 6in (15cm). Separate the strands of the starting yarns to give a "feather duster" effect.
I make these 2 st with the 2.25mm crochet hook. If you have difficulty with this, use a larger crochet hook or make the tail with only 1 yarn (white or black).

BODY

In black. Crochet in the round, in closed rounds.
Rnd 1: 6 sc in a magic circle (6 st).
Rnd 2: 6 inc (12 st).
Rnd 3: 1 sc, 1 inc) x 6 (18 st).
Rnd 4: (1 sc, 1 inc, 1 sc) x 6 (24 st).
In white.
Rnd 5: 24 sc in the BLO (24 st).
In black.
Rnd 6: 24 sc (24 st).
In white.
Rnd 7: 24 sc (24 st).
In black.
Rnds 8 and 9: Repeat rnds 6 and 7, using the colors indicated (24 st).
In black, make and attach the back legs to the body as explained in the instructions for the Body in the *Basic Shapes* section, p. 30.
Rnd 10: (1 sc, 1 dec, 1 sc) x 6. Change color to white (18 st).
Rnd 11: (1 sc, 1 dec) x 6 (12 st).
Cut off the yarn, keeping a length of 4in (10cm). Do not close yet.
Sew the tail to the back side, between rnds 4 and 5: insert the needle in the 1st st of rnd 5, from the outside to the inside of the body, and bring the needle out again to the side, in the last st of rnd 5. Thread the yarns through the 2nd ch of the tail, from the front to the back, and insert the needle into the body, between the 2 sewing stitches. Tie the yarns in a knot on the inside and cut them off.
In black, make and attach the front feet to the body as explained in the Assembly part of the *Basic Shapes* section, p. 31.
Then follow the rest of the instructions in that part to finish the zebra.

Leopard

3 hours

pp. 6–7

Dimensions
Approximate height: 2⅝in (6cm)

Materials
- One 2.25mm crochet hook
- DMC Happy Cotton (¾oz–47yd [20g–43m]), shade 775, black, 7/100oz (2g); shade 794, mustard, 4/10oz (11g); shade 777, brown, 7/100oz (2g); shade 762, white, 39in (1m); shade 764, pale pink, 12in (30cm)
- Two 6mm (¼in) safety eyes

EARS x 2

In mustard.
Row 1: 6 sc in a magic circle, ch 1 (6 st).
Turn the piece 180 degrees, and crochet the 1st st of row 2 in the last st of row 1.
Row 2: 6 sc (6 st).
Cut the yarn to a length of 8in (20cm).

MUZZLE

In white. Crochet in a spiral.
Rnd 1: 6 sc in a magic circle (6 st).
Rnd 2: 1 inc, 2 sc, 1 sc and 1 sl st in the same st.
Do not crochet the last st (8 st).
Cut the yarn to a length of 10in (25cm).

HEAD

In mustard. Crochet in a spiral.
Rnd 1: 6 sc in a magic circle (6 st).
Rnd 2: 2 inc, 1 sc; in brown: 1 sc in the same st; in black: 1 sc; in mustard: 1 sc in the same st; 2 inc (12 st).
Rnd 3: (1 sc, 1 inc) x 4, 2 sc; in brown: 1 sc in the same st; in black: 1 sc; in mustard: 1 inc (18 st).
Rnd 4: 2 sc; in brown: 1 sc in the same st; in black: 1 sc; in mustard: 1 sc, 1 inc; in brown: 1 sc; in black: 1 sc; in mustard: 1 inc, 3 sc; in brown: 1 sc in the same st; in black: 1 sc; in mustard: (1 sc, 1 inc, 1 sc) x 2 (24 st).
Rnd 5: (7 sc, 1 inc) x 2, 8 sc; in brown: 1 sc in the same st (27 st).
Rnd 6: In black: 1 sc; in mustard: 2 sc, 1 inc, 8 sc; in brown: 1 sc; in black: 1 sc in the same st; in mustard: 8 sc, 1 inc, 5 sc (30 st).
Rnd 7: (In mustard: 8 sc; in brown: 1 sc; in black: 1 sc) x 2; in mustard: 6 sc; in brown: 1 sc; in black: 1 sc; in mustard: 2 sc (30 st).
Rnd 8: 2 sc; in brown: 1 sc; in black: 1 sc; in mustard: 26 sc (30 st).
Rnd 9: (In mustard: 6 sc; in brown: 1 sc; in black: 1 sc) x 3; in mustard: 5 sc; in brown: 1 sc (30 st).
Rnd 10: In black: 1 sc; in mustard: 29 sc (30 st).
Rnd 11: 3 sc; in brown: 1 dec; in black: 1 sc; in mustard: 2 sc, 1 dec, (3 sc, 1 dec) x 3; in brown: 1 sc; in black: 1 sc; in mustard: 1 sc, 1 dec (24 st).
Insert the safety eyes between rnds 9 and 10, in st 12 and 19 of rnd 9.
Sew the ears on each side of the head, straddling rnds 4 and 5. Make a sewing stitch in the 1st and last st of rnd 2 of the ear, as well as in the hollow of the ear.
Bring the starting yarn inside the head. Tie the yarns on the inside and cut them off.
Start to stuff the head.
Rnd 12: (1 sc, 1 dec, 1 sc) x 2; in brown: 1 sc; in black: 1 dec; in mustard: 2 sc, 1 dec; in brown: 1 sc; in black: 1 sc; in mustard: 1 dec, 2 sc, 1 dec, 1 sc (18 st).
Rnd 13: (1 dec, 1 sc) x 5, 1 dec, 1 sl st (12 st).
Cut the yarn to a length of 12in (30cm).

Finish stuffing the head. Sew the muzzle between the eyes, straddling rnds 10 and 11 of the head. The 2 st of the first rnd not crocheted in rnd 2 of the muzzle must be positioned toward the top.
With the pink yarn, embroider a little horizontal line just above the first rnd of the muzzle.
If you wish, embroider or draw the cheeks according to the instructions given in the *Basic Shapes* section, p. 30.

TAIL

In mustard. Crochet in a spiral.
Rnd 1: 4 sc in a magic circle (4 st).
Rnd 2: 1 inc, 1 sc; in black: 1 sc; in brown: 1 sc. Tie the black and brown starting yarns together (5 st).
Rnd 3: In mustard: 5 sc (5 st).
Rnd 4: 1 sc; in black: 1 sc; in brown: 1 sc; in mustard: 2 sc (5 st).
Rnd 5: 4 sc; in black: 1 sc (5 st).
Rnd 6: In brown: 1 sc; in mustard: 4 sc (5 st).
Rnd 7: 2 sc; in black: 1 sc; in brown: 1 sc; in mustard: 1 sc. Stop the black and brown yarns (5 st).
Rnd 8: 4 sc, 1 sl st (5 st).
Cut the mustard yarn to a length of 8in (20cm).
If you find it difficult to make the color changes on this narrow piece, it is possible to make the tail entirely in mustard.

BODY

The body is crocheted in the round, in closed rnds. The sl st that closes each rnd and the ch that starts each rnd are not indicated in the instructions, for better readability, but you must make them for each rnd. For more instructions, see the *Techniques* chapter, p. 24.
In mustard. Crochet in the round, in closed rnds.
Rnd 1: 6 sc in a magic circle (6 st).
Rnd 2: 6 inc (12 st).
Rnd 3: (1 sc, 1 inc) x 6 (18 st).
Rnd 4: (1 sc, 1 inc, 1 sc) x 6 (24 st).
Rnd 5: 24 sc in the BLO (24 st).
Rnd 6: (In mustard: 1 sc; in black: 1 sc; in brown: 1 sc; in mustard: 3 sc) x 4 (24 st).
Rnd 7: 24 sc (24 st).
Rnd 8: (In mustard: 4 sc; in black: 1 sc; in brown: 1 sc) x 4 (24 st).
Rnd 9: In mustard: 24 sc (24 st).
In mustard, make the back feet and attach them to the body as explained in the instructions for the Body in the *Basic Shapes* section, p. 30.
Rnd 10: (In black: 1 sc; in brown: 1 dec; in mustard: 2 sc, 1 dec; in black: 1 sc; in brown: 1 sc; in mustard: 1 dec, 1 sc) x 2 (18 st).
Rnd 11: (1 sc, 1 dec) x 6 (12 st).
Cut the yarn, keeping a 4in (10cm) length.
Do not close the body yet.
Sew the tail to the back, straddling rnds 5 and 6 of the body. Tie the yarn in a knot on the inside and cut it off.
In mustard, make the front feet and attach them to the body as explained in the Assembly section of *Basic Shapes*, p. 31. Then follow the rest of the instructions in that part to finish the leopard.

Ostrich

 2 hours 45 minutes

 pp. 6, 8

Dimensions
Approximate height: 4in (10cm)

Materials
› One 2.25mm crochet hook
› DMC Happy Cotton (¾oz–47 yd [20g–43m]), shade 773, beige, 1/10oz (3g); shade 761, ecru, 4½yd (4m); shade 764, pale pink, 1/7oz (4g); shade 775, black, 1/7oz (4g)
› DMC Pearl Cotton Size 5, shade 310, black, 12in (30cm)
› Two 6mm (¼in) safety eyes

BEAK

In pink. Crochet in a spiral.
Rnd 1: 4 sc in a magic circle (4 st).
Rnd 2: (1 inc, 1 sc) x 2 (6 st).
Rnd 3: 1 sl st. Do not crochet the other st (6 st).
Cut the yarn to a length of 10in (25cm). Flatten the beak so as to have the yarn at one end.

HEAD AND BODY

Head

In beige. Crochet in a spiral.
Rnd 1: 6 sc in a magic circle (6 st).
Rnd 2: 6 inc (12 st).
Rnd 3: (1 sc, 1 inc) x 6 (18 st).
Rnd 4: (4 sc, 1 inc, 1 sc) x 3 (21 st).
Rnds 5 to 7: 21 sc (21 st).
Insert the safety eyes between rnds 5 and 6, in st 8 and 14 of rnd 5. Before putting the washers on the back of the safety eyes, embroider two little eyelashes in black Pearl Cotton, toward the outside of each eye. Each eyelash starts from the st in which the safety eye is inserted and goes 1 st toward the outside, and 1 rnd higher for the 2nd eyelash.
Rnd 8: (4 sc, 1 dec, 1 sc) x 3 (18 st).
Sew the beak between the eyes, between rnds 6 and 7. Tie the yarn in a knot on the inside and cut it off.
Start stuffing the head.
Rnd 9: 9 dec (9 st).
Finish stuffing the head. Make sure to stuff it enough in spite of its small size.

Neck

Rnd 10: 1 dec, 5 sc, 1 dec (7 st).
Stuff the neck as you go along.
Rnds 11 to 13: 7 sc (7 st).
In ecru. Stop the beige yarn.
Rnd 14: 7 sc (7 st).

Body

In black. Stop the ecru yarn.
Rnd 15: 2 sc; ch 5, 1 sc in the 2nd st away from the crochet hook; continuing along the ch: 3 sc; 1 sc in the next st of rnd 14, 1 sc, 2 inc, 1 sc (13 st).
Verify that the head and the start of the body are lined up correctly. Depending on how you crochet, it may be slightly offset.
The ch must be at the back of the body, well centered with respect to the position of the eyes. If this is not the case, add or subtract 1 sc at the start of rnd 15. In order to avoid losing your place in the instructions, mark the sc that precedes the one where the ch starts as being the 1st st of rnd 15.
Rnd 16: 2 sc; going back up the length of the ch: 3 sc, 1 inc; coming back down the other side of the ch: (1 inc, 1 sc) x 2; 7 sc (20 st).
Rnd 17: 3 sc, 1 inc, 1 sc, 4 inc, 3 sc, 1 inc, 7 sc (26 st).
Rnd 18: 2 sc, 1 inc, 23 sc (27 st).
Rnd 19: (1 sc, 1 dec, 6 sc) x 3 (24 st).
Rnd 20: (5 sc, 1 dec, 1 sc) x 3 (21 st).

Rnd 21: (1 sc, 1 dec, 4 sc) x 3 (18 st).
Start stuffing the body.
Rnd 22: (1 sc, 1 dec) x 6 (12 st).
Rnd 23: 6 dec (6 st).
Finish stuffing and close.

FEET x 2

In pink. Crochet in a spiral.
Rnd 1: 5 sc in a magic circle (5 st).
Rnds 2 to 9: 5 sc (5 st).
Rnd 10: 2 sc, 2 sl st. Do not crochet the other st. (6 st).
Cut the yarn, keeping 10in (25cm) of length.

WINGS x 2

In black. Crochet in a spiral.
Rnd 1: 6 sc in a magic circle (6 st).
Rnd 2: (1 sc and 2 hdc) in 1 st, mark the 1st hdc, (2 hdc and 1 sc) in the next st. Do not crochet the other st (10 st).
Cut the yarn to a length of 10in (25cm). Stop it invisibly and keep the rest of the yarn for sewing the wing to the body.
In ecru.
Pull a strand of yarn through the st marked on rnd 2, keeping 4in (10cm) of yarn at the start, and do the following: ch 1; (1 sc and 1 hdc) in the next st; ch 2, 1 sl st in the 2nd st away from the crochet hook; (1 hdc and 1 sc) in the next black st; 1 sl st in the next st.
Cut the yarn to a length of 4in (10cm). Stop this yarn and the starting yarn by making an invisible knot and bringing the yarns under a few st before cutting them off flush with the surface.

TAIL

In ecru. Crochet in a spiral.
Rnd 1: Ch 4, 2 sc in the 2nd st away from the crochet hook; continuing along the ch: 1 sc; in the last st of the ch: 3 sc; coming back up the other side of the ch: 2 sc (8 st).
Rnd 2: 8 sc (8 st).
Rnd 3: 1 sl st. Do not crochet the other st (8 st).
Cut the yarn to a length of 10in (25cm).

ASSEMBLY

Sew the wings on by centering them on each side of the body. The first black rnd must straddle rnds 18 to 20 of the body, while the ecru point lies toward the back of the body. With the black ending yarn, sew all around the black part. The ecru part of the wings remains free. Bring the yarn to the inside and cut it off flush with the surface.
Sew the legs spaced 1 st apart, centering them at the front of the body, between rnds 20 and 21.
Sew the tail on the back of the body, straddling rnds 17 and 18. Before making the last sewing stitches, adjust the stuffing.
If you wish, embroider or draw cheeks according to the instructions given in the *Basic Shapes* section, p. 30.

Giraffe

 3 hours 30 minutes

 pp. 6, 9

Dimensions
Approximate height: 3½in (9cm)

Materials
- One 2.25mm crochet hook
- DMC Happy Cotton (¾oz–47yd [20g–43m]), shade 770, lemonade yellow, 7/20oz (10g); shade 761, ecru, 20in (50cm)
- DMC Lumina (¾oz–164yd [20g–150m]), shade L677, pink gold, 19yd (17m)
- Divide 16yd (15m) into three equal lengths. Crochet the parts in pink gold by using these three yarns simultaneously, to produce a thickness similar to that of Happy Cotton. The rest of the length will be used for the embroidery.
- Two 4.5mm (1/5in) safety eyes

EARS x 2

In yellow. Crochet in a spiral.
Rnd 1: 4 sc in a magic circle (4 st).
Rnd 2: (1 inc, 1 sc) x 2 (6 st).
Rnd 3: (1 inc, 1 sc) x 3 (9 st).
Rnd 4: 4 dec, 1 sl st (5 st).
Cut the yarn to a length of 8in (20cm). Flatten the ear so that this yarn is at one end.
With the ecru yarn, embroider two small vertical lines 1 rnd high in the middle of each ear. I prefer to embroider beside the 1st and 2nd st of rnd 4 so that the ear will be sewn in the right orientation.
Tie knots in the yarns, cut them off, and bring the ends inside the ear.

HORNS x 2

In gold.
Ch 3, keeping 4in (10cm) of starting yarn; 2 sc in the 2nd st away from the crochet hook; 1 sl st in the next st of the ch.
Cut the yarn to a length of 4in (10cm).

MUZZLE

In gold. Crochet in a spiral.
Rnd 1: Ch 4, 2 sc in the 2nd st away from the crochet hook; continuing along the ch: 1 sc; in the last st of the ch: 3 sc; coming back up the other side of the ch: 2 sc (8 st).
Rnd 2: 8 sc (8 st).
Rnd 3: 1 sl st. Do not crochet the other st (8 st).
Cut the yarn to a length of 10in (25cm).

HEAD AND BODY

Head

In yellow. Crochet in a spiral.
Rnd 1: 6 sc in a magic circle (6 st).
Rnd 2: 6 inc (12 st).
Rnd 3: (1 sc, 1 inc) x 6 (18 st).
Rnd 4: (4 sc, 1 inc, 1 sc) x 3 (21 st).
Rnds 5 to 7: 21 sc (21 st).
Insert the safety eyes between rnds 5 and 6, in st 8 and 14 of rnd 5.
Sew the ears on each side of the head, straddling rnds 3 and 4. Sew the horns, bringing the starting and ending yarns through each side of rnd 1 of the head. Tie the yarns in a knot on the inside and cut them off.
Rnd 8: (4 sc, 1 dec, 1 sc) x 3 (18 st).
Sew the muzzle between the eyes, straddling rnds 6 and 7. Tie the yarns in a knot on the inside and cut them off.
Start stuffing the head.
Rnd 9: 9 dec (9 st).
Finish stuffing the head. Make sure to add enough stuffing in spite of its small size.

Neck

Rnd 10: 1 dec, 5 sc, 1 dec (7 st).
Stuff the neck as you go along.
Rnds 11 to 15: 7 sc (7 st).
Rnd 16: 6 sc; in the FLO: 1 inc (8 st).

Body

Rnd 17: In FLO: 3 inc; in both loops: 1 sc, 1 inc, 2 sc, 1 inc (13 st).
Verify that the head and the start of the body are lined up well. Depending on how you crochet, they may be slightly offset.
The 4 inc of rnds 16 and 17 must be at the back, well centered with respect to the position of the eyes.
If that is not the case, adjust or remove 1 sc in rnd 16 before doing the inc. In order to keep your place in the instructions, mark the 3rd st of the 4 successive inc as the 1st st of rnd 17.
Rnd 18: 5 inc, 8 sc (18 st).
Rnd 19: 18 sc (18 st).
Rnd 20: 1 sc, 7 inc, 10 sc (25 st).
Rnd 21: 19 sc, 2 dec, 2 sc (23 st).
Rnd 22: 6 sc, (1 sc, 1 inc) x 2, 9 sc, 1 dec, 2 sc (24 st).
Rnd 23: (1 sc, 1 dec, 1 sc) x 6 (18 st).
Rnd 24: (1 dec, 1 sc) x 6 (12 st).
Start stuffing the body.
Rnd 25: 6 dec (6 st).
Finish stuffing and close.

FEET x 4

In gold. Crochet in a spiral and stuff as you go along.
Rnd 1: 4 sc in a magic circle (4 st).
Rnd 2: 1 inc, 3 sc (5 st).
In yellow. Stop the gold yarn.
Rnds 3 to 5: 5 sc (5 st).
Rnd 6: 4 sc, 1 sl st (5 st).
Cut the yarn, saving 10in (25cm) of length.

TAIL

In gold.
Ch 4, keeping 6in (15cm) of starting yarn; 3 sl st along the ch, starting with the 2nd st away from the crochet hook.
Cut the yarn to a length of 6in (15cm).
Using a needle, thread an 8in (20cm) length of yellow yarn through the end of the tail, on the opposite side from the starting and ending yarns. Make an overhand knot with the two halves of the yellow yarn, and tighten it well, as close as possible to the tail. Cut the yarns to a length of 1/5in (1cm) and separate the strands to give a feather duster effect to the end of the tail.

ASSEMBLY

Use pins to position the four feet before sewing them, to make sure that the giraffe is not wobbly.
I place the front feet on each side of the neck (2 or 3 st of distance between them), straddling rnd 21 of the body. The back legs are placed straddling rnd 24, with about 2 st of distance between them. Sew on each foot, then bring the yarn to the inside and cut it off flush with the surface.

Sew the tail between the 2 back legs, between rnds 22 and 23 of the body.
If you wish, embroider or draw the cheeks according to the instructions given in the *Basic Shapes* section, p. 30.
With a doubled gold yarn, embroider triangle patterns on different parts of the body, neck, and head.

Peacock

 3 hours

 p. 10

Dimensions
Approximate height: 2¾in (7cm)
Approximate length: 4in (10cm)

Preliminary information
The body and the feathers are crocheted in the round, in closed rounds. The sl st that closes each rnd and the ch that starts each rnd are not indicated in the instructions, for better readability, **but you must make them for each rnd**. For more instructions, see the *Techniques* chapter, p. 24.

Materials
- One 2.25mm crochet hook
- DMC Happy Cotton (¾oz–47yd [20g–43m]), shade 798, royal blue, 7/20oz (10g); shade 779, apple green, 4/10oz (12g); shade 784, Tiffany blue (aqua), 2¼yd (2m); shade 772, tan, 2¼yd (2m); shade 762, white, 20in (50cm); shade 794, mustard, 20in (50cm)
- DMC Lumina (¾oz–164yd [20g–150m]), shade L3821, gold, 16yd (15m)
- Divide this length into three equal pieces. Crochet the parts in gold by using these three yarns simultaneously, to produce a thickness similar to that of Happy Cotton.
- Two 6mm (¼in) safety eyes

CREST

In royal blue.
Ch 4, keeping 4in (10cm) of starting yarn; 1 sc in the 2nd st away from the crochet hook, and 2 sl st continuing along the ch.
Continue by making a 2nd ch of ch 4; 1 sc in the 2nd st away from the crochet hook, 2 sl st continuing along the ch.
Cut the yarn to a length of 4in (10cm).
This forms two feathers of the same size that will be sewn to the top of the head.

BEAK

In tan. Crochet in a spiral.
Rnd 1: 4 sc in a magic circle (4 st).
Rnd 2: 1 inc, 3 sc (5 st).
Rnd 3: 2 sc, 1 inc, 2 sc (6 st).
Rnd 4: 1 sl st. Do not crochet the other st. (6 st).
Cut the yarn to a length of 8in (20cm). Stuff lightly.

HEAD

In royal blue, follow the instructions in *Basic Shapes* for Head B, p. 30.
After rnd 11, sew the crest to the top of the head. Use the ending yarn to sew it straddling the 1st rnd. Bring the starting yarn to the inside, tie the two yarns together on the inside of the head, and cut them off.
Using a needle and 8in (20cm) of white yarn, embroider three small lines around each plastic eye. The first line, the longest, is placed above the eye and close to it. Each of the other two lines starts from one end of the first line and ends at a point below and to the inside of the eye, forming the lower inside corner of the eye.
Tie the yarns in a knot on the inside.
Finish crocheting the head.
If you wish, embroider or draw the cheeks according to the instructions given in the *Basic Shapes* section, p. 30.

WINGS x 2

In royal blue. Crochet in a spiral.
Rnd 1: 6 sc in a magic circle (6 st).
Rnd 2: (1 sc, 1 hdc) in 1 st, (2 dc, ch 2, 1 sl st in the 2nd st away from the crochet hook, 2 dc) in 1 st, (1 hdc, 1 sc) in 1 st, 1 sl st. Do not crochet the other st (11 st).
Cut the yarn to a length of 10in (25cm).

TRAIN

In apple green. Crochet in a spiral.
Rnd 1: 6 sc in a magic circle, keeping 12in (30cm) of starting yarn (6 st).
Rnd 2: 6 inc (12 st).
Rnd 3: (1 sc, 1 inc) x 6 (18 st).
Rnd 4: (1 sc, 1 inc, 1 sc) x 6 (24 st).
Rnd 5: (3 sc, 1 inc) x 6 (30 st).
Rnd 6: (2 sc, 1 inc, 2 sc) x 6 (36 st).
Rnd 7: (5 sc, 1 inc) x 6 (42 st).
Rnd 8: (3 sc, 1 inc, 3 sc) x 6 (48 st).
Rnd 9: (7 sc, 1 inc) x 6 (54 st).
Rnd 10: (4 sc, 1 inc, 4 sc) x 6 (60 st).
Rnd 11: (9 sc, 1 inc, 5 sc) x 6 (66 st).
Rnd 12: (5 sc, 1 inc, 5 sc) x 6 (72 st).
Rnd 13: (11 sc, 1 inc) x 6 (78 st).
Make 1 sl st, ch 1, and fold the piece in half to crochet the two thicknesses together.
Start by inserting the crochet hook in the next st and in the st that precedes the sl st, and make 1 sc.
Continue crocheting the two thicknesses: (1 picot, 1 sc in the next st) x 37.
To make a picot, ch 3, then 1 sl st in the 3rd st away from the crochet hook.
Stop the yarn and cut it off.

EYE FEATHERS x 5

In royal blue. Crochet in the round, in closed rounds.
Rnd 1: In a magic circle: 1 sc in royal blue, 5 sc in Tiffany blue (6 st).
In gold.
Rnd 2: 6 inc (12 st).
Close rnd 2 with a sl st and cut the ending gold yarns to a length of 12in (30cm). Tie the starting blue yarns and the starting gold yarns in a knot on the back side and cut them off short
Sew the eye feathers on one side of the tail, straddling the 4 next-to-last rnds of the tail.
Before sewing, position the 5 eye feathers with pins to make sure that they are uniformly distributed over the surface. Bring the sewing yarns to the inside and cut them off.

BODY

In royal blue. Crochet in the round, in closed rnds.
Rnd 1: 6 sc in a magic circle (6 st).
Rnd 2: 6 inc (12 st).
Rnd 3: (1 sc, 1 inc) x 6 (18 st).
Rnd 4: 18 sc in the BLO (18 st).
Rnd 5: 18 sc (18 st).
In mustard, make the back legs and attach them as explained in the instructions for the Body in the *Basic Shapes* section, p. 30. Since the body is finer here, sew the 1st leg in st 7 and 8 of rnd 3 and the 2nd leg in st 11 and 12 of rnd 3 (between rnds 3 and 4).
Rnd 6: (1 sc, 1 inc, 1 sc) x 6 (24 st).
Rnd 7: 24 sc (24 st).
Rnd 8: (1 sc, 1 dec, 1 sc) x 6 (18 st).
Rnds 9 and 10: 18 sc (18 st).
Rnd 11: (1 sc, 1 dec) x 6 (12 st).
Sew the wings on each side of the body.
Sew only around the first rnd of the wings, straddling rnds 9 and 10 of the body.
With the apple green yarn from the start of the train, sew the train to the back of the body, making sure that it is nice and straight so that the peacock will rest correctly on the ground. Sew over 5 rnds of height (rnds 4 to 8 of the body), on each side of the line of sl st that close the rnds of the body.
Bring the yarn to the inside and cut it off flush with the surface.
Follow the instructions of the Assembly part of the *Basic Shapes* section, p. 31, to finish the peacock.

Frog

 2 hours 15 minutes

 p. 10

Dimensions
Approximate height: 2⅝in (6.5cm)

Materials
- One 2.25mm crochet hook
- DMC Happy Cotton (¾oz–47yd [20g–43m]), shade 782, almond green (or 781 malachite green), 7/20oz (10g); shade 788, lemon yellow, 2¼yd (2m); shade 762, white, 12in (30cm)
- DMC Pearl Cotton Size 5, shade 310, black, 12in (30cm)
- Optional, to replace the yellow: DMC Lumina (¾oz–164yd [20g–150m]), shade L3821, gold, 6½yd (6m). Divide this length into three equal pieces. Crochet the parts in gold using these three yarns simultaneously, to produce a thickness similar to that of Happy Cotton.
- Two 4.5mm (1/5in) safety eyes

EYES x 2

In green. Crochet in a spiral.
Rnd 1: 6 sc in a magic circle (6 st).
Rnd 2: 6 inc (12 st).
Rnd 3: 12 sc (12 st).
Rnd 4: (1 sc, 1 dec, 1 sc) x 2, 1 sc, 1 dec, 1 sl st (9 st).
Cut the yarn to a length of 10in (25cm) and tighten the last sl st well.
Insert one safety eye between rnds 3 and 4, in st 5 of rnd 3. Using a needle and 6in (15cm) of white yarn, embroider a short line above the eye, as close as possible to the plastic eye.
Tie the ends of the yarn on the inside, then add a little stuffing to each side of the stem of the safety eye. *If you find it difficult to insert the safety eyes, it is possible to use little black beads, sewn on with black thread.*

CROWN

In yellow or gold. Crochet in a spiral.
Rnd 1: Ch 6, keeping 12in (30cm) of starting yarn, and make a ring by making a sl st in the 1st st of the ch; 8 sc in the starting ring thus formed (8 st).
Rnd 2: 8 sc (8 st).
Rnd 3: (1 sc, 1 picot, 1 sl st in the next st) x 4.
Cut the yarn to a length of 6in (15cm) and stop it invisibly. *To make a picot, ch 3, then 1 sl st in the 3rd st away from the crochet hook.*

HEAD

In green. Crochet in a spiral.
Rnd 1: 6 sc in a magic circle (6 st).
Rnd 2: 6 inc (12 st).
Rnd 3: (1 sc, 1 inc) x 6 (18 st).
Rnd 4: (1 sc, 1 inc, 1 sc) x 6 (24 st).
Rnd 5: (7 sc, 1 inc) x 3 (27 st).
Rnds 6 to 9: 27 sc (27 st).
Rnd 10: (7 sc, 1 dec) x 3 (24 st).
Rnd 11: (1 sc, 1 dec, 1 sc) x 6 (18 st).
Start stuffing the head.
Rnd 12: (1 dec, 1 sc) x 5, 1 dec, 1 sl st (12 st).
Cut the yarn to a length of 12in (30cm). Finish stuffing the head.

BODY

In green, follow the instructions for the Body in *Basic Shapes*, p. 30.
Once the head has been sewn to the body, sew on the remaining elements: sew the crown at the level of rnd 1 of the head with the starting yarn.
When finished, bring the yarn back inside and secure these yarns by making several stitches in the head before cutting the yarn off flush with the surface.
Sew the eyes to the head, on each side of the crown, straddling rnds 3 to 5. Bring the yarns inside and cut them off flush with the surface.

Using a needle and black Pearl Cotton, embroider the mouth across rnds 6 to 8, making three small lines, one after the other, like this:

If you wish, embroider or draw the cheeks straddling rnd 6 of the head, following the instructions given in the *Basic Shapes* section, p. 30.

Panda

 2 hours 30 minutes

 p. 11

Dimensions
Approximate height: 2⅓in (6cm)

Materials
- One 2.25mm crochet hook
- Happy Cotton (¾oz–47 yd [20g–43m]), shade 775, black, 1/5oz (5g); shade 762, white, ¼oz (7g); shade 764, pale pink, 20in (50cm)
- Two 6 mm (¼in.) safety eyes

EARS x 2

In black. Crochet in a spiral.
Rnd 1: 6 sc in a magic circle (6 st).
Rnd 2: 6 inc (12 st).
Rnd 3: (1 sc, 1 dec, 1 sc) x 3 (9 st).
Rnd 4: 1 sl st, do not crochet the other st of the rnd (8 st).
Cut the yarn to a length of 10in (25cm). Flatten the ear so as to have the yarn at one end and curve it inward slightly.

HEAD

In white, follow instructions for Head A in the *Basic Shapes* section, p. 30.
After rnd 11, sew the ears so that they straddle rnds 4 to 6, curving them slightly inward.
Tie the yarns in a knot on the inside of the head and cut them off.
With 12in (30cm) of black yarn, embroider the eye patches under each eye by making three small lines close to the plastic eye and close to each other.
Make the nose in the form of a triangle straddling rnd 10. The following diagram indicates the lines to be embroidered:

Tie the yarns in a knot and cut them off, then finish crocheting the head.
If you wish, you can embroider or draw the cheeks according to the instructions given in the *Basic Shapes* section, p. 30.

TAIL

In white.
In a magic circle, keeping 4in (10cm) of starting yarn, make: 1 sc, 2 hdc, 1 sc.
Cut the yarn to a length of 6in (15cm).

BODY

Follow the instructions for the Body in the *Basic Shapes* section, p. 30. Make the body in white, with the exception of the last 3 rnds (rnds 9 to 11), which must be made in black (the color change is done when you make the last sc of rnd 8). The front and back legs are made in black.
With the ending yarn, sew the 1st and last st of the tail 1 st apart at the back of the body. Tie the starting and ending yarns in a knot on the inside of the body and cut them off.
With 10in (25cm) of pink yarn, embroider a little heart straddling rnd 10. To do that, embroider a V, doubling each branch of the V. Tie the yarns in a knot on the inside of the body.

Monkey

 2 hours 45 minutes

 p. 11

Dimensions
Approximate height: 2⅓in (6cm)

Materials
- One 2.25mm crochet hook
- DMC Happy Cotton (¾oz–47yd [20g–43m]), shade 773, beige, 4/100oz (12g); shade 761, ecru, 7/100oz (2g)
- DMC Lumina (¾oz–164yd [20g–150m]), shade L677, pink gold, 14yd (12m). Divide this length into three equal pieces. Crochet the parts in pink gold by using these three yarns simultaneously, to produce a thickness similar to that of Happy Cotton.
- Polyester plush effect yarn 22/25oz–93yd [25g–85m]), shade white, 39in (1m)
- DMC Pearl Cotton Size 5, shade 310, black, 39in (1m)
- Two 6mm (¼in) safety eyes
- Chenille stem, 4in (10cm)

EARS x 2

Inside part x 2
In ecru.
5 sc in a magic circle. Cut the yarn to a length of 4in (10cm). Using a needle, thread the yarn under both loops of the 1st st made in the magic circle, from the back to the front. Then thread this yarn under the BL of the last st made in the circle, from the front to the back.
Tie this yarn to the starting yarn and cut it off.
You now have a closed circle with 6 st.

Outside part x 2
In beige. Crochet in a spiral.
Rnd 1: 6 sc in a magic circle (6 st).
Rnd 2: Crochet the two parts simultaneously, positioning the ecru circle over the beige one.
For the entire rnd, you will insert the crochet hook in the BLO of the st from the ecru part, and in both loops of the beige part: 5 inc, 1 sc (11 st).
Rnd 3: Cut the yarn to a length of 10in (25cm). If the starting yarn is still visible, bring the starting yarn of the beige part to the inside of the ear and cut it off flush with the surface.

MUZZLE

In ecru. Crochet in a spiral.
Rnd 1: Ch 3, 1 inc in the 2nd st away from the crochet hook; in the last st of the ch: 3 sc; coming back up the other side of the ch: 1 sc (6 st).
Rnd 2: 6 inc (12 st).
Rnd 3: 12 sc (12 st).
Rnd 4: 1 sl st. Do not crochet the other st (12 st).
Cut the yarn to a length of 10in (25cm).

HEAD

In beige. Crochet in a spiral.
Rnd 1: 6 sc in a magic circle (6 st).
Rnd 2: 6 inc (12 st).
Rnd 3: (1 sc, 1 inc) x 6 (18 st).
Rnd 4: (1 sc, 1 inc, 1 sc) x 6 (24 st).
Rnd 5: (7 sc, 1 inc) x 3 (27 st).
Rnd 6: 3 sc, 1 inc, 6 sc; in ecru: 2 sc; in beige: 1 inc, 1 sc; in ecru: 2 sc; in beige: 5 sc, 1 inc, 5 sc (30 st).
Rnds 7 to 9: 11 sc; in ecru: 8 sc; in beige: 11 sc (30 st).
Rnd 10: 12 sc; in ecru: 6 sc; in beige: 12 sc (30 st).
Rnd 11: (3 sc, 1 dec) x 6 (24 st).
Insert the safety eyes between rnds 8 and 9, in st 13 and 18 of rnd 9.
Start stuffing the head.

Rnd 12: (1 sc, 1 dec, 1 sc) x 6 (18 st).
Rnd 13: (1 dec, 1 sc) x 5, 1 dec, 1 sl st (12 st).
Cut the yarn to a length of 12in (30cm).
Finish stuffing the head. Sew the muzzle in place between the eyes, straddling rnds 9 to 11 of the head.
Sew the ears on each side of the head, at the height of the eyes, 4 st to the outside of each eye. Make a sewing stitch in the last st crocheted and in the following one.
To keep the ears from folding toward the front, make 1 sewing stitch in the st at the back of each ear to keep it in place.
Bring the yarn to the inside and cut it off.
With the Pearl Cotton, embroider eyebrows over rnd 7. Then, on the muzzle, embroider two small lines as nostrils between rnds 2 and 3 on the top side, and a mouth below, between rnds 1 and 2.
If you wish, embroider or draw cheeks according to the instructions given in the *Basic Shapes* section, p. 30.

TAIL

In pink gold.
Rnd 1: 4 sc in a magic circle (4 st).
Rnd 2: 1 inc, 3 sc (5 st).
Rnds 3 and 4: 5 sc (5 st).
In beige.
Rnds 5 to 16: 5 sc (5 st).
Rnd 17: 4 sc, 1 sl st (5 st).
Cut the yarn to a length of 8in (20cm).
Take a chenille stem and bend back one end using pliers. Insert the bent end into the tail, up to the tip of the tail. Bend the chenille stem at the length desired and cut it off 4/10in (1cm) farther away. Bring the chenille stem out again, just far enough that you can finish folding the end, and put it back in the tail using the pliers.

BODY

In beige.
Follow the instructions for the Body in the *Basic Shapes* section, p. 30.
Sew the tail to the back side, straddling rnds 5 and 6 of the body. Tie a knot in the yarn on the inside and cut it off.

Hat

Pom-pom

With the plush yarn. Crochet in a spiral.
You can use a 2.5mm crochet hook to work more easily with this yarn.
Rnd 1: 6 sc in a magic circle (6 st).
Rnd 2: 6 sc (6 st).
Cut the yarn to a length of 4in (10cm). Close the pom-pom and keep the starting and ending yarns.

Hat

In pink gold. crochet in a spiral.
Rnd 1: 6 sc in a magic circle (6 st).
Rnd 2: (1 sc, 1 inc, 1 sc) x 2 (8 st).
Using a needle, thread the two plush yarns of the pom-pom through the magic circle to the inside of the hat. Tie these yarns together with the starting yarn of the hat, pulling the knot tight.
Rnd 3: (3 sc, 1 inc) x 2 (10 st).
Rnd 4: (2 sc, 1 inc, 2 sc) x 2 (12 st).
Rnd 5: (1 inc, 5 sc) x 2 (14 st).
Rnd 6: (3 sc, 1 inc, 3 sc) x 2 (16 st).
Cut the yarn to a length of 12in (30cm). Sew the hat on the monkey's head, straddling rnd 1 and rnds 2 to 4 on one side of the head. Add a little stuffing before making the last stitches. Bring the yarns to the inside and cut them off flush with the surface.

Hen

 2 hours 30 minutes

 p. 12

Dimensions
Approximate height: 2⅝in (6.5cm)

Materials
› One 2.25mm crochet hook
› DMC Happy Cotton (¾oz–47yd [20g–43m]), shade 776, camel, ¼oz (7g); shade 777, brown, ⅕oz (5g); shade 789, red, 3⅓yd (3m); shade 788, lemon yellow, 2¼yd (2m)
› Two 6mm (¼in) safety eyes

COMB

In red.
Ch 10, keeping 12in (30cm) of starting yarn; (1 hdc and 1 dc) in the 3rd st away from the crochet hook, ch 2, 1 sl st in the next st on the ch; *ch 1, (1 hdc and 1 dc) in the same st, ch 2, 1 sl st in the next st*.
Repeat from * to * twice more, to form 4 rounded contours in all.
Cut the yarn to a 6in (15cm) length.

BEAK

In yellow. Crochet in a spiral.
Rnd 1: 5 sc in a magic circle (5 st).
Rnd 2: (1 inc, 1 sc) x 2, 1 inc (8 st).
Rnd 3: 1 sl st. Do not crochet the other st (8 st).
Cut the yarn to a length of 8in (20cm).

WATTLES x 2

In red.
Ch 2, keeping 6in (15cm) of starting yarn; (1 sc and 1 sl st) in the 2nd st away from the crochet hook.
Cut the yarn to a length of 6in (15cm).

HEAD

In camel, follow the instructions for Head B in the *Basic Shapes* section, p. 30.
Sew the beak in place between the two eyes, straddling rnds 10 and 11 of the head.
Insert the needle at the back of the head, centering it well, between rnds 5 and 6. Bring the needle out again at the front of the head, in the middle, between rnds 3 and 4.
Make 1 sewing stitch at the end before the comb. Once the comb is positioned, sew the entire starting ch to the head, then bring the yarn out under the head, through the stuffing.
Likewise, bring the starting yarn of the comb to the inside of the head, tie them together, and cut them off.
Sew the wattles under the beak this way: bring the starting yarn and the ending yarn through the same st and bring them out again under the head. Tie 1 strand of yarn from the right wattle to 1 strand of yarn from the left wattle and tighten the knot well. Do the same thing with the other strands of yarn, and then cut them off.
If you wish, embroider or draw the cheeks according to the instructions given in the *Basic Shapes* section, p. 30.

WINGS x 2

In camel.
Ch 6, keeping 4in (10cm) of starting yarn: 1 hdc in the 3rd st away from the crochet hook; continuing along the ch: 1 dc, 2 tr.
Cut the yarn to a length of 8in (20cm).

TAIL

In brown.
Ch 8, keeping 4in (10cm) of starting yarn: 1 sc in the 2nd st away from the crochet hook; continuing along the ch: 1 sc, 1 picot, 1 hdc, 1 picot, 1 dc, 1 picot,

1 hdc, 1 picot, 1 sc, 1 sl st.
Cut the yarn to a length of 10in (25cm).
To make a picot, ch 3, then 1 sl st in the 3rd ch away from the crochet hook.

BODY

In brown. Crochet in the round, in closed rounds. The sl st that closes each rnd and the ch that starts each rnd are not indicated in the instructions, for better readability, but you must make them for each rnd. For more instructions, see the *Techniques* chapter, p. 24.
Rnd 1: 6 sc in a magic circle (6 st).
Rnd 2: 6 inc (12 st).
Rnd 3: (1 sc, 1 inc) x 6 (18 st).
Rnd 4: (1 sc, 1 inc, 1 sc) x 6 (24 st).
Rnd 5: 24 sc in the BLO (24 st).
Rnds 6 to 9: 24 sc (24 st).
In yellow, make the back legs and attach them to the body as explained in the instructions for the body in the *Basic Shapes* section, p. 40.
In camel. Stop the brown yarn.
Rnd 10: (1 long sc, 1 dec, 1 long sc) x 6 (18 st).
To make 1 long sc, the technique is the same as for making 1 sc, except for where you insert the crochet hook. Instead of inserting the crochet hook under the 2 loops of a st of the preceding rnd, as is usually done, insert the crochet hook under the 2 loops of a st made 2 rows before (in this case, rnd 8), and pull 1 loop as high as the other st of the rnd that you are in the process of crocheting.
Rnd 11: (1 sc, 1 dec) x 6 (12 st).
With the ending yarn, sew on the tail, making a sewing stitch in each one of the 7 st of the base ch. Sew the ends between rnds 4 and 5, in the 1st and the last st of rnd 5, and the other st of the ch above, forming an upside-down U. Tie the starting and ending yarns in a knot inside the body and cut them off.
Sew the wings on each side of the body.
Thread a needle with one of the wing yarns and insert the needle between the 2 long st above the feet, between rnds 9 and 10. Insert the other yarn 3 st toward the back, between rnds 10 and 11 of the body. Make some sewing stitches along the upper part of the wings and leave the bottom part free.
To finish the hen, follow the instructions for Assembly in the *Basic Shapes* section, p. 30.

Chick

1 hour 30 minutes

p. 12

Dimensions
Approximate height: 2⅓in (6cm)

Materials
- One 2.25mm crochet hook
- DMC Happy Cotton (¾oz–47yd [20g–43m]), shade 787, vanilla, ⅓oz (9g); shade 753, tangerine orange, 60in (1.5m); shade 762, white, 1/7oz (4g).
- DMC Lumina (¾oz–164yd [20g–150m]), shade L3821, gold, 60in (1.5m). Divide this length into two equal pieces. Crochet the knot using these two yarns simultaneously.
- Two 6mm (¼in) safety eyes

HEAD

In vanilla, follow the instructions for Head B in the *Basic Shapes* section, p. 30.
Using a needle and 8in (20cm) of orange yarn, embroider the beak as shown, making the upper line 1 rnd under the line of the eyes:

If you wish, embroider or draw the cheeks according to the instructions given in the *Basic Shapes* section, p. 30.

WINGS x 2

In vanilla.
In a magic circle, keeping 4in (10cm) of starting yarn, make: ch 1, 1 hdc, 3 dc, 1 hdc, 1 sl st.
Cut the yarn to a length of 6in (15cm).

BODY

Make the body in vanilla and the legs in orange, following the instructions for the Body in the *Basic Shapes* section, p. 30.
Sew the wings on each side of the body, straddling rnd 10. Make a sewing stitch at the level of the 1st and the last st of each wing. Bring the starting yarn to the inside. Tie the two yarns together on the inside and cut them off.

SHELL

In white. Crochet in a spiral.
Rnd 1: 6 sc in a magic circle (6 st).
Rnd 2: (1 inc, 2 sc) x 2 (8 st).
Rnd 3: (1 sc, 1 inc) x 4 (12 st).
Stop the starting yarn and cut it off flush with the surface.
Rnd 4: (1 sc, 1 inc, 1 sc) x 4 (16 st).
Rnd 5: (3 sc, 1 inc) x 4 (20 st).
Rnd 6: (2 sc, 1 inc, 2 sc) x 4 (24 st).
Rnd 7: (5 sc, 1 inc) x 4 (28 st).
Rnd 8: (3 sc, 1 inc, 3 sc) x 4 (32 st).
Rnd 9: (7 sc, 1 inc) x 4 (36 st).
Rnd 10: (1 sc, 1 hdc, 1 dc, 1 hdc, 1 sc, 1 sl st, 1 sc, 1 dc, 1 tr, 1 dc, 1 sc, 1 sl st) x 3 (36 st).
Cut the yarn to a length of 4in (10cm). Stop the yarn invisibly. Tie the yarn in a subtle knot on the inside, thread it under several st to stop it, then cut it off flush with the surface.

Knot

In gold.
In a magic circle, make: (Ch 2, 1 dc, ch 2, 1 sl st) x 2.
Close the magic circle, then with the ending yarns, make several turns around the center of the shape obtained, tightening it well. Tie the starting and ending yarns together on the back.
Sew the knot wherever you want to on the shell, then tie the yarns together on the back side, and pass them under a few st before cutting them off flush with the surface.

Lamb

 3 hours

 p. 13

Dimensions
Approximate height: 2⅝in (6.5cm)

Materials

› One 2.25mm crochet hook and one 2.5mm crochet hook
› DMC Happy Cotton (¾oz–47yd [20g–43m]), shade 762, white, ⅕oz (5g); shade 773, beige, ¼oz (7g); shade 764, pale pink, 10in (25cm)
› Polyester plush effect yarn (22/25oz–93yd [25g–85m]), shade white, ⅐oz (4g)
› Two 6mm (¼in) safety eyes

EARS x 2

In beige. Crochet in a spiral with the 2.25mm crochet hook.
Rnd 1: 6 sc in a magic circle (6 st).
Rnd 2: (1 inc, 1 sc) x 3 (9 st).
Rnd 3: 9 sc (9 st).
Rnd 4: (1 dec, 1 sc) x 2, 1 dec, 1 sl st (6 st).
Cut the yarn to a length of 10in (25cm). Flatten the ear so as to have the yarn at one end.

FLEECE

With the plush effect yarn and the 2.5mm crochet hook. Crochet in a spiral.
Rnd 1: 6 sc in a magic circle (6 st).
Rnd 2: 6 inc (12 st).
Rnd 3: (1 sc, 1 inc) x 6 (18 st).
Rnd 4: (1 sc, 1 inc, 1 sc) x 6 (24 st).
Rnd 5: (7 sc, 1 inc) x 3 (27 st).
Rnd 6: (3 sc, 1 inc, 5 sc) x 3 (30 st).
Rnds 7 to 11: 30 sc (30 st).
Rnd 12: 1 sl st, do not crochet the other st (30 st).
Cut the yarn to a length of 16in (40cm).

HEAD

In beige, with the 2.25mm crochet hook, follow the instructions for Head A in the *Basic Shapes* section, p. 30.
After stuffing the head, place the fleece on the head: at the back, it is placed over rnd 12, and in front, over rnd 6.
Pin the fleece to the head, then sew all around with the ending yarn to keep the fleece in place.
Sew the ears on each side of the head.
Sew both thicknesses simultaneously, making 3 sewing stitches for each ear.
Bring the yarns out through the stuffing under the head, and tie the two yarns together.
With 10in (25cm) of pink yarn, embroider a Y to represent the muzzle, straddling rnds 10 and 11.
If you wish, embroider or draw cheeks according to the instructions in the *Basic Shapes* section, p. 30.

TAIL

In beige. Crochet in a spiral with the 2.25mm crochet hook.
Rnd 1: 7 sc in a magic circle (7 st).
Rnd 2: 2 sc, 1 dec, 3 sc (6 st).
Rnd 3: 1 sl st. Do not crochet the other st. (6 st).
Cut the yarn to a length of 8in (20cm). Flatten the tail so as to have the yarn at one end.

BODY

In white, with the 2.25mm crochet hook.
Crochet in the round, in closed rnds. The sl st that closes each rnd and the ch that starts each rnd are not indicated in the instructions, for better readability, but they must be done for each rnd.
For more instructions, see the *Techniques* chapter, p. 24.
Rnd 1: 6 sc in a magic circle (6 st).
Rnd 2: 6 inc (12 st).
Rnd 3: (1 sc, 1 inc) x 6 (18 st).
Rnds 4 to 9: In the BLO: 18 sc. Mark the FL of the 1st st of rnd 4 (18 st).

In beige, make the back legs and attach them as explained in the instructions for the Basic Shapes, p. 30. Since the body is thinner here, sew the 1st leg in st 5 and 7 of rnd 3 and the 2nd leg in st 12 and 14 of rnd 3 (between rnds 3 and 4).
Sew the tail at the back, between rnds 3 and 4. Sew both thicknesses of the tail at the same time, making 2 sewing stitches.
Tie the yarn in a knot on the inside and cut it off.
Rnd 10: In the BLO: (1 sc, 1 dec) x 6 (12 st).
The decreases are made by flowing 2 st together. For more instructions, see the Techniques *chapter, p. 24.*
Cut the yarn to a length of 4in (10cm). Do not close yet.
In beige, make the front legs and attach them to the body as explained in the Assembly part of the *Basic Shapes* section, p. 31. Since the body is thinner here, sew the 1st leg in st 6 and 7 of rnd 8 and the 2nd leg in st 13 and 14 of rnd 8 (between rnds 8 and 9).
With the plush effect yarn and the 2.5mm crochet hook, pull a yarn through the previously marked st, ch 1, and follow the instructions below, starting to crochet in the same st, and crocheting in the FL that remain visible. This part is crocheted in a spiral, and the ch made at the end of each rnd serves to reach the 1st st of the following round.
Rnds 5b to 8b: (1 sc, 1 inc, 1 sc) x 6, ch 1 (24 st).
Rnds 9b and 10b: 18 sc (18 st).
Cut the yarn to a length of 4in (10cm). Bring the starting and ending yarns inside the body and tie them in a knot on the inside.
Then follow the rest of the instructions for the Assembly part of the *Basic Shapes* section, p. 31, to finish the lamb.

Mouse

p. 13

Dimensions
Approximate height: 2⅝in (6.5cm)

Materials
- One 2.25mm crochet hook
- DMC Happy Cotton (¾oz–47yd [20g–43m]), shade 757, pearl gray, 7/20oz (10g); shade 768, old rose, 2¼yd (2m)
- DMC Lumina (¾oz–164yd [20g–150m]), shade L3821, gold, 5½yd (5m). Divide this length into two equal pieces. Crochet the scarf using these two yarns simultaneously.
- Two 6mm (¼in) safety eyes

EARS x 2

Inside part x 2
In pink.
5 sc in a magic circle. Cut the yarn to a length of 4in (10cm). Using a needle, thread this yarn under the 2 loops of the 1st st made in the magic circle, from the back to the front. Then thread this yarn under the BL of the last st made in the circle, from the front to the back.
Tie this yarn to the starting yarn and cut it off.
You will have a closed circle with 6 st.

Outside part x 2
In gray. Crochet in a spiral.
Rnd 1: 6 sc in a magic circle (6 st).
Rnd 2: Crochet the two parts simultaneously, positioning the pink circle over the gray one. Insert the crochet hook in the BLO of the pink part and in both loops of the gray part: 5 inc, do not crochet the last st of the rnd (10 st).

HEAD

In gray, follow the instructions for Head A in the *Basic Shapes* section, p. 30.
After rnd 11, sew an ear on each side of the head, straddling rnds 4 and 6. Make a sewing stitch in the 1st and last st of rnd 2 of the ear, as well as in the st not crocheted, between them. Bring the starting yarn back into the head. Tie the yarns on the inside and cut them off.
Finish crocheting the head.
With 8in (20cm) of pink yarn, embroider a short line of two or three thicknesses between rnds 10 and 11, between the two eyes, to represent the muzzle.
If you wish, embroider or draw the cheeks according to the instructions given in the *Basic Shapes* section, p. 30.

TAIL

In gray.
Ch 7, keeping ⅖in (1cm) of starting yarn. Pull the starting knot tight. Cut the ending yarn to a length of 6in (15cm). Separate the strands of the starting yarn to give a "feather duster" effect.

BODY

In gray, follow the instructions for the Body in the *Basic Shapes* section, p. 30.
Once the body is done, sew the tail to the back side, between rnds 4 and 5: insert the needle in the 1st st of rnd 5, from the outside to the inside of the body, and bring the needle out to the side, in the last st of rnd 5. Thread the yarn through the 7th ch of the tail, from the front to the back, and then into the body, between the 2 sewing stitches.
Tie the yarn in a knot on the inside and cut it off.

SCARF

In gold. Ch 40, keeping 4in (10cm) of starting yarn, then 39 sc in the ch starting from the 2nd st away from the crochet hook. Cut the yarn to a length of 3in (10cm).
Tie the starting and ending yarns together and pull them under a few st of the scarf before cutting them off flush with the surface.

Bee

Dimensions
Approximate height: 2⅓in (6cm)

Materials

- One 2.25mm crochet hook
- DMC Happy Cotton (¾oz–47yd [20g–43m]), shade 777, brown, ¼oz (7g); shade 794, mustard, ⅐oz (4g); shade 762, white, 3¼yd (3m)
- Two 6mm (¼in) safety eyes

HEAD

In brown, follow the instructions for Head A in the *Basic Shapes* section, p. 30.
Thread a needle with a length of brown yarn 12in (30cm) long, and add the antennae: insert the needle on one side of the head between rnds 4 and 5, and bring it out again on the other side of the head, at the same height. Make a knot in the yarn, close to the head, on each side of the head, to keep the antennae in place. Then make another knot on each antenna, at the height of the eye. Cut the yarn, leaving about ⅖in (1cm) of yarn beyond each knot.
If you wish, embroider or draw the cheeks according to the instructions given in the *Basic Shapes* section, p. 30.

WINGS

In white. Crochet in a spiral around the starting ch.
Rnd 1: Ch 16, keeping 6in (15cm) of starting yarn, 2 hdc in the 3rd st away from the crochet hook; continuing along the ch: 3 dc, 1 hdc, 1 sc, 1 sl st, 1 sc, 1 hdc, 3 dc; in the st at the end of the ch: 4 hdc; coming back up the other side of the ch: 3 dc, 1 hdc, 1 sc, 2 sl st, 1 sc, 1 hdc, 3 dc; 2 hdc in the last st (32 st).
Rnd 2: 7 sl st, make the next 2 sl st above those made in rnd 1, inserting the crochet hook again in the starting ch; 14 sl st; 2 sl st above those of rnd 1; 7 sl st.
Cut the yarn to a length of 10in (25cm). Stop the yarn invisibly, then pull it under the st of rnd 1, bringing it out again at the level of the 1st central sl st.
Also thread the starting yarn under the st up to the center of the wings. Keep the yarns to sew with.

BODY

In brown. Crochet in the round, in closed rnds. The sl st that closes each rnd and the ch that starts each rnd are not indicated in the instructions, for better readability, but you must make them for each rnd. For more instructions, see the *Techniques* chapter, p. 24.
To make color changes invisible at the end of a rnd, they are to be done during the last sc of the rnd; this means that the sl st and the ch that end the rnd and start the next rnd are to be done in the new color.
Rnd 1: 6 sc in a magic circle (6 st).
Rnd 2: 6 inc (12 st).
Rnd 3: (1 sc, 1 inc) x 6 (18 st).
Rnd 4: (1 sc, 1 inc, 1 sc) x 6 (24 st).
Rnd 5: 24 sc in the BLO.
Change color to mustard (24 st).
Rnds 6 and 7: 24 sc. At the end of rnd 7, change color to brown (24 st).
Rnd 8: 24 sc. Change color to mustard (24 st).
Rnd 9: 24 sc (24 st).
In brown, make the back legs and attach them to the body as explained in the instructions for the Body, in the *Basic Shapes* section, p. 30.
Rnd 10: (1 sc, 1 dec, 1 sc) x 6. Change color to brown (18 st).
Rnd 11: (1 sc, 1 dec) x 6 (12 st).
Cut the yarn to a length of 4in (10cm). Do not close the body yet.

Sew the wings on the back, placing the starting ch between rnds 8 and 9. Make 6 sewing stitches in the center of this starting ch, and then tie the yarns in a knot on the inside and cut them off. I tighten the tension of the yarns threaded along the st when sewing them, to make the wings more rigid. Make sure not to tighten them too much, though, to avoid pulling the wings out of shape.

In brown, make the front legs and attach them to the body as explained in the Assembly part of the *Basic Shapes* section, p. 31. Then follow the rest of the instructions in that part to finish the bee.

Ladybug

2 hours

 p. 15

Dimensions
Approximate height: 2⅓in (6cm)

Materials

- One 2.25mm crochet hook
- DMC Happy Cotton (¾oz–47yd [20g–43m]), shade 775, black, 7/20oz (10g); shade 789, red, 5½yd (5m)
- Two 6mm (¼in) safety eyes

HEAD

In black, follow the instructions for Head A in the *Basic Shapes* section, p. 30.

With 12in (30cm) of black yarn, add the antennae: insert the needle on one side of the head, between rnds 4 and 5, and bring it out again on the other side of the head, at the same height. Make a knot in the yarn on each side of the head, close to the head, to hold the antennae in place. Then make another knot in each antennae, at the level of the eye. Cut the yarns off about 2/5in (1cm) below each knot.

To make the cheeks, with red yarn, embroider a short line with two thicknesses of yarn below and to the outside of each eye.

WINGS x 2

In red. Crochet in a spiral.

Rnd 1: 6 sc in a magic circle (6 st).

Rnd 2: 6 inc (12 st).

Rnd 3: (1 sc, 1 inc) x 6 (18 st).

Rnd 4: 1 sl st. Do not crochet the other st (18 st).

Cut the yarn to a length of 12in (30cm) and tighten the last sl st well. Fold the wing in half, keeping the yarn at one end. Using a needle and the ending yarn, sew the BL of the st of rnd 3 of each wing edge to edge in this way: insert the needle in the BL of the first st of rnd 3, from the outside to the inside, then insert the needle in the BL of the 1st st of rnd 3 (the one in which you made the sl st of rnd 4). This forms the 1st sewing stitch on the wing. Make 8 more sewing stitches in the same way, so that the bottom of the wing is completely closed. Keep the yarn for sewing.

With an 8in (20cm) length of black yarn, embroider three black spots on the face of one of the red circles. Tie the yarns on the back of the wing (this side will be sewn against the body). Embroider the three black spots on the other wing on the side opposite to the one embroidered on the 1st wing.

BODY

In black, follow the instructions for the Body in the *Basic Shapes* section, p. 30.

Sew the wings to the back. The upper part of each wing is placed between rnds 10 and 11, in the 1st and last st of rnd 10. The lower part of each wing is positioned diagonally, 2 st toward the outside with respect to the upper part. Make several sewing stitches on each wing so that it is well attached over its entire surface. Tie the yarn in a knot on the inside and cut it off.

Snail

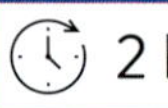 2 hours

 p.16

Dimensions
Approximate height: 2¾in (7 cm)

Materials
- One 2.25mm crochet hook and one 2.5mm crochet hook
- DMC Happy Cotton (¾oz–47yd [20g–43m]), shade 771, curry ⅓oz (9g); shade 750, teal blue, 1/10oz (3g); shade 767, splash blue, 1/7oz (4g)
- DMC Pearl Cotton Size 5, shade 310, black, 8in (20cm)
- Two 4.5mm (1/5in) safety eyes

SHELL

In teal blue, with a 2.25mm crochet hook.
Crochet in a spiral. Stuff lightly as you go along.
Rnd 1: 5 sc in a magic circle (5 st).
Rnd 2: 1 inc, 4 sc (6 st).
From rnd 3 to the end, crochet in the BLO.
Rnd 3: 1 sc, 1 inc, 4 sc (7 st).
Rnd 4: 1 sc, 2 inc, 2 sc, 1 dec (8 st).
Rnd 5: 2 sc, 1 inc, 5 sc (9 st).
Rnd 6: 3 sc, 2 inc, 3 sc, 1 dec. This last dec is made by inserting the crochet hook in the last st of rnd 5, and in the first st of the next rnd (rnd 6). Mark the following sc as being the 1st st of the next rnd (10 st).
The dec indicated at the end of rnds 8, 10, 12, and 14 are also done straddling the 2 rnds.
Likewise, mark the following st as the 1st st of the next rnd.
Rnd 7: 3 sc, 1 inc, 6 sc (11 st).
Rnd 8: 4 sc, 2 inc, 4 sc, 1 dec (12 st).
Rnd 9: 4 sc, 1 inc, 7 sc (13 st).
Rnd 10: 5 sc, 2 inc, 5 sc, 1 dec (14 st).
Rnd 11: 5 sc, 1 inc, 8 sc (15 st).
Rnd 12: 6 sc, 2 inc, 6 sc, 1 dec (16 st).
Rnd 13: 6 sc, 1 inc, 9 sc (17 st).
Rnd 14: 7 sc, 2 inc, 7 sc, 1 dec (18 st).
Rnd 15: 1 sl st. Mark the FL of this st.
Do not crochet the other st (18 st).
Cut the yarn to a length of 12in (30cm).
With a 2.5mm crochet hook, pull a splash blue yarn through the FL of the previously marked st, inserting the crochet hook from the bottom of the horn that you just crocheted toward the top. Keep 4in (10cm) of starting yarn and stop it on the back side. Ch 1, then 1 sc in the FL of the next st, and in each FL going back up in a spiral until you reach the top of the horn. Make 1 sl st in the FL of the last st.
Cut the yarn to a length of 12in (30cm). Imagine a vertical line joining this last sl st to the inc of rnd 14. Using a yarn needle, thread the ending yarn under the sl st made in relief along this vertical line. Then pull as hard as you can on this yarn to curve the horn inward, to give it the shape of a spiral snail shell. Bring the point of the shell to the level of the 1st rnd of st in relief and make several stitches through the shell, pulling them tight, to maintain the shell in this position. Once the shell is solidly secured, stop the yarn.

ANTENNAE x 2

In curry, with a 2.25mm crochet hook.
Ch 5, crocheting loosely, keeping 4in (10cm) of starting yarn.
Make 4 sl st crocheted tightly, starting at the 2nd st away from the crochet hook.
Cut the yarn to a length of 4in (10cm).

HEAD AND BODY

Head
In curry, with a 2.25mm crochet hook.
Crochet in a spiral.
Rnd 1: 6 sc in a magic circle (6 st).

Rnd 2: 6 inc (12 st).
Rnd 3: (1 sc, 1 inc) x 6 (18 st).
Rnd 4: (4 sc, 1 inc, 1 sc) x 3 (21 st).
Rnd 5: (1 sc, 1 inc, 5 sc) x 3 (24 st).
Rnds 6 to 8: 24 sc (24 st).
Rnd 9: 3 sc, 3 dec, 6 sc, 3 dec, 3 sc (18 st).
Insert the safety eyes between rnds 6 and 7, in st 10 and 15 of rnd 6.
Sew the antennae on each side of the head, inserting the starting and ending yarns between rnds 3 and 4. Make sure that they curve toward the front. Tie the yarns in a knot on the inside and cut them off.
Start stuffing the head.
Rnd 10: (1 sc, 4 dec) x 2 (10 st).
Rnd 11: 3 sc, 1 dec, 2 sc, 1 dec, 1 sc (8 st).
Finish stuffing the head. Do not stuff it too firmly.
With Pearl Cotton, embroider a little mouth in a V, between the eyes, straddling rnd 8.
If you wish, embroider or draw the cheeks according to the instructions given in the *Basic Shapes* section, p. 30.

Body
Do not stuff the body.
Rnd 12: In the FLO: 8 sc (8 st).
Rnd 13: (3 sc, 1 inc) x 2 (10 st).
Rnd 14: (4 sc, 1 inc) x 2 (12 st).
Rnds 15 and 16: 12 sc (12 st).
Rnd 17: (3 sc, 1 inc) x 3 (15 st).
Rnds 18 to 27: 15 sc (15 st).
Rnd 28: (3 sc, 1 dec) x 3 (12 st).
Rnd 29: 6 dec (6 st).
Rnd 30: 6 sc (6 st).
Close. Flatten the body.
Sew the shell with the ending teal blue yarn, straddling rnds 21 to 27 of the body.
Before stopping the yarn, make a little invisible sewing stitch to maintain the head against the shell. Insert the needle between rnds 7 and 8 of the head, and between the 4th and 5th rnds in relief on the shell, starting from the bottom.

Butterfly

 2 hours 30 minutes

 p. 17

Dimensions
Approximate height:
2⅓in (6cm)

Materials

› One 2.25mm crochet hook
› DMC Happy Cotton (¾oz–47yd [20g–43m]), shade 768, old rose, 3/10 oz (8g); shade 764, pale pink, 3/10oz (3g); shade 783, pale green, ¼oz (7g)
› DMC Lumina (¾oz–164yd [20g–150m]), shade L3821, gold, 8¾yd (8m). Divide this length into two equal pieces. Crochet the parts in gold using both yarns simultaneously.
› Two 6mm (¼in) safety eyes

HEAD

In old rose, follow the instructions for Head A in the *Basic Shapes* section, p. 30.
In old rose, make 2 chains of ch 10 each, cutting off the ending yarn at a length of 6in (15cm). With the ending yarn, sew these two antennae on each side of the head between rnds 4 and 5. Tie the yarns in a knot on the inside and cut them off. Cut the starting yarns to a length of 2/5in (1cm) from the starting slip knot.
If you wish, embroider or draw the cheeks according to the instructions given in the *Basic Shapes* section, p. 30.

WINGS x 2

Lower part x 2

In pale green. Crochet in a spiral.
Rnd 1: 6 sc in a magic circle (6 st).
Rnd 2: (1 inc, 2 sc) x 2 (8 st).
Stop the yarn invisibly, and mark the false st thus created.

Upper part x 2

In pale green. Crochet in a spiral. Do not stuff.
Rnd 1: 5 sc in a magic circle (5 st).
Rnd 2: 1 inc, 4 sc (6 st).
Rnd 3: (1 inc, 1 sc) x 3 (9 st).
Rnd 4: (1 sc, 1 inc, 1 sc) x 3 (12 st).
Rnd 5: (3 sc, 1 inc) x 3 (15 st).
Rnd 6: 15 sc (15 st).
Rnd 7: 14 sc, 1 sl st (15 st).
Attach the two parts together, making 1 sl st in the previously marked st on the lower part. Now crochet all around these two parts as if it were one piece (skipping the 2 st that join the two parts). Mark the following st as the 1st st of rnd 8.
Rnd 8: 1 sc in the next st of the lower part, 6 sc, 14 sc around the upper part (21 st).
Rnd 9: 7 sc, (1 dec, 4 sc) x 2, 1 dec (18 st).
Rnd 10: 7 sc, 1 dec, 3 sc, 1 dec, 2 sc, 1 dec (15 st).
Rnd 11: 7 sc, (1 dec, 1 sc) x 2, 1 dec (12 st).
Rnd 12: 6 dec (6 st).
Cut the yarn to a length of 10in (25cm). Flatten the wing.

Large gold eyespot x 2

In gold. Crochet in a spiral.
Rnd 1: 6 sc in a magic circle (6 st).
Rnd 2: 3 inc, (1 sc, 1 hdc) in 1 st, (1 dc, ch 2, 1 sl st in the 2nd st away from the crochet hook, 1 dc) in 1 st, (1 hdc, 1 sc) in 1 st (12 st).
Rnd 3: 1 sl st. Do not crochet the other st (12 st).
Cut the yarns to a length of 12in (30cm), and sew this piece on the upper part of the wing, straddling rnds 3 to 9. On the 2nd wing, this piece must be sewn on the face opposite to the 1st wing.

Small gold eyespot x 2
In gold. Crochet in a spiral.
Make 5 sc in a magic circle. Cut the yarns to a length of 10in (25cm). Using a needle, thread these yarns under the two loops of the 1st st made in the magic circle, from the back to the front. Then thread these yarns under the BL of the last st made in the circle, from the front to the back. You should have a closed circle with 6 st.
Using the ending yarns, sew this piece on the lower part of the wing, at 2 rnds from the magic circle. On the 2nd wing, this piece must be sewn on the side opposite to the one on the 1st wing.

BODY

In old rose. Crochet in the round, in closed rnds. The sl st that closes each rnd and the ch that starts each rnd are not indicated in the instructions, for better readability, but you must make them for each rnd. For more instructions, see the *Techniques* chapter, p. 24.
To make color changes invisible at the end of a rnd, they are to be done when making the last sc of the rnd; this means that the sl st and the ch that end the rnd and start the next rnd are to be made in the new color.
Rnd 1: 6 sc in a magic circle (6 st).
Rnd 2: 6 inc (12 st).
Rnd 3: (1 sc, 1 inc) x 6 (18 st).
In pale pink.
Rnd 4: 18 sc in the BLO (18 st).
In old rose.
Rnd 5: 18 sc (18 st).
In old rose, make the back legs and attach them as explained in the instructions for the Body in the *Basic Shapes* section, p. 30. Since the body is finer here, sew the 1st leg in st 7 and 8 of rnd 3 and the 2nd leg in st 11 and 12 of rnd 3 (between rnds 3 and 4).
In pale pink.
Rnd 6: (1 sc, 1 inc, 1 sc) x 6 (24 st).
In old rose.
Rnd 7: 24 sc (24 st).
In pale pink.
Rnd 8: (1 sc, 1 dec, 1 sc) x 6 (18 st).
In old rose.
Rnd 9: 18 sc (18 st).
In pale pink.
Rnd 10: 18 sc (18 st).
In old rose.
Rnd 11: (1 sc, 1 dec) x 6 (12 st).
Sew the wings to the back of the body, straddling rnds 7 to 9, centering them over the line formed by the sl st that close each rnd. Sew the last 6 st of each wing, flat, by inserting the needle through both thicknesses, one placed on top of the other. Tie the yarns in a knot at the back and cut them off.
To finish the butterfly, follow the instructions for the Assembly part of the *Basic Shapes* section, p. 31.

Ray

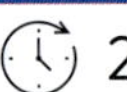 2 hours 30 minutes

 p. 18

Dimensions
Approximate dimensions: 3 3/20in x 4⅛in (8cm x 10.5cm), including the tail

Materials
› One 2.25mm crochet hook
› DMC Happy Cotton (¾oz–47yd [20g–43m]), shade 750, teal blue, 2/5oz (12g); shade 762, white, 1/10oz (3g)
› Two 6mm (¼in) safety eyes
› Chenille stem, 4in (10cm)

LOBES x 2

In teal blue.
Ch 3, keeping 4in (10cm) of starting yarn. 1 sl st in the 2nd st away from the crochet hook, 1 sc in the following st.
Cut the yarn to a length of 4in (10cm).

BODY

In teal blue. Crochet in a spiral.
Rnd 1: Make 1 chain of ch 9, 1 sc in the 2nd st away from the crochet hook; continuing along the ch: 6 sc; in the last st of the ch: 3 sc; coming back up the other side of the ch: 6 sc, 1 inc (18 st).
Rnd 2: (8 sc, 1 inc) x 2 (20 st).
Rnd 3: (8 sc, 1 dec) x 2 (18 st).
Rnd 4: 9 sc, *ch 7, 1 sc in the 2nd st away from the crochet hook; continuing along the ch: 5 sc*; 1 inc in the next st of rnd 3, 8 sc, then repeat the sequence between * * (31 st).
Rnd 5: 1 inc in the 1st st of rnd 4, 7 sc, 1 inc; *coming back up the length of the ch: 5 sc and 1 inc; returning to the st of rnd 4: 1 inc, 5 sc*, 9 sc, 1 inc; repeat the sequence between * * (50 st).
Insert the safety eyes between rnds 2 and 3, in st 12 and 17 of rnd 2.
Sew the lobes between rnds 1 and 2, in st 9 and 18 of rnd 1. Bring the starting and ending yarns to the inside and tie them in knots on the inside. Start to stuff the ray's head, between the stems of the safety eyes.
Rnd 6: 50 sc (50 st).
Rnd 7: 16 sc, 2 dec, 21 sc, 2 dec, 5 sc (46 st).
Rnd 8: (1 dec, 7 sc, 1 dec, 4 sc, 2 dec, 4 sc) x 2 (38 st).
Rnd 9: 12 sc, 2 dec, 15 sc, 2 dec, 3 sc (34 st).
Rnd 10: 10 sc, 3 dec, 11 sc, 3 dec, 1 sc (28 st).
Rnd 11: 9 sc, 3 dec, 8 sc, 3 dec. The 3rd dec is made by inserting the crochet hook in the last st of rnd 10 and the 1st st of rnd 11. Mark the following st as the 1st st of rnd 12 (22 st).
Rnd 12: (7 sc, 2 dec) x 2 (18 st).
Rnd 13: 18 sc (18 st).
Stuff the body only, keeping the fins quite flat. Stuff lightly; the body must not be too firm.
Rnd 14: 9 dec (9 st).
Rnd 15: (1 sc, 1 dec) x 3 (6 st).
Finish stuffing the body.
Rnd 16: 1 dec, 4 sc (5 st).
Rnds 17 to 26: 5 sc (5 st).
Rnd 27: 4 sc, 1 sl st (5 st).
Cut the yarn to a length of 6in (15cm).
Take a chenille stem and bend over one end using pliers. Use a piece long enough for the chenille stem to run the full length of the tail and enter a little way inside the body. Fold the end over using pliers, then cut it off. Insert the chenille stem in the tail, up to the end.
Close the tail and bring the yarn to the inside.

BELLY

In white. Crochet in rows. The dec of this part will be done by flowing 2 st together.
For more instructions, see the *Techniques* chapter, p. 24.

Row 1: Ch 9, keeping 20in (50cm) of starting yarn, 1 sc in the 2nd st away from the crochet hook; continuing along the ch: 7 sc, turn (8 st).
Row 2: Ch 1, 8 sc, turn (8 st).
Row 3: Ch 1, 8 sc, 8 ch, turn (16 st).
Row 4: Starting with the 2nd st away from the crochet hook: 15 sc, 8 ch, turn (23 st).
Row 5: Starting in the 2nd st away from the crochet hook: 22 sc, turn (22 st).
Row 6: Ch 1, skip the 1st st, 6 sc, 1 dec, 13 sc, turn (20 st).
Row 7: Ch 1, skip the 1st st, 6 sc, 1 dec, 8 sc, 1 dec, 1 sc, turn (17 st).
Row 8: Ch 1, skip the 1st st, 13 sc, 1 dec, 1 sc, turn (15 st).
Row 9: Ch 1, skip the 1st st, 11 sc, 1 dec, 1 sc, turn (13 st).
Row 10: Ch 1, skip the 1st st, 9 sc, 1 dec, 1 sc, turn (11 st).
Row 11: Ch 1, skip the 1st st, 7 sc, 1 dec, 1 sc, turn (9 st).
Row 12: Ch 1, skip the 1st st, 5 sc, 1 dec, 1 sc, turn (7 st).
Row 13: Ch 1, skip the 1st st, 6 sc, turn (6 st).
Row 14: Ch 1, skip the 1st st, 2 sc, 1 dec, 1 sc, turn (4 st).
Row 15: Ch 1, skip the 1st st, 2 sc, 1 sl st (3 st).
Cut the yarn to a length of 20in (50cm).
Position the belly under the ray, considering that the 1st and last rows are the place of the work, so as to position the belly in the right orientation. Sew all around the belly, using the starting and ending yarns for each half of the perimeter. Pull the yarns to the inside and cut them off flush with the surface.
If you wish, embroider or draw the cheeks according to the instructions given in the *Basic Shapes* section, p. 30.

Baby Seal

1 hour 45 minutes

p. 19

Dimensions
Approximate length: 3¼in (8cm)

Materials
- One 2.25mm crochet hook
- DMC Happy Cotton (¾oz–47yd [20g–43m]), shade 762, white, 4/10oz (11g); shade 759, gray, 2¼yd (2m)
- DMC Pearl Cotton Size 5, shade 310, black, 39in (1m)
- Two 6mm (¼in) safety eyes

FEET x 2

In white. Crochet in a spiral.
Rnd 1: Ch 4, 1 sc in the 2nd st away from the crochet hook, 1 sc in the next st; in the last st of the ch: 3 sc; coming back up the other side of the ch: 1 sc, 1 inc (8 st).
Rnds 2 and 3: 8 sc (8 st).
Rnd 4: 1 sc, 1 dec, 2 sc, 1 dec, 1 sl st (6 st).
Cut the yarn to a length of 10in (25cm).

BODY

Body

In gray. Crochet in a spiral.
Rnd 1: 6 sc in a magic circle (6 st).
Rnd 2: 3 sc, 3 inc (9 st).
In white. Stop the gray yarn.
Rnd 3: 9 sc (9 st).
Rnd 4: 9 inc (18 st).
Rnd 5: 18 sc (18 st).
Rnd 6: (1 sc, 1 inc) x 6, 6 sc (24 st).
Rnd 7: (1 sc, 1 inc, 1 sc) x 6, 6 sc (30 st).
Rnds 8 to 10: 30 sc (30 st).
Insert the safety eyes between rnds 6 and 7, in st 5 and 14 of rnd 6. With the black yarn, embroider a small black line 1 st in width and with several thicknesses, over 1 st of rnd 2, between the eyes. Tie a knot on the back side.
Rnd 11: (7 sc, 1 inc, 2 sc) x 3 (33 st).
Rnd 12: 33 sc (33 st).
Rnd 13: (7 sc, 1 dec, 2 sc) x 3 (30 st).
Rnd 14: 30 sc (30 st).
Rnd 15: (5 sc, 1 dec) x 3, 9 sc (27 st).
Rnd 16: 7 sc, 1 dec, 4 sc, 1 dec, 9 sc, 1 dec, 1 sc (24 st).
Rnd 17: 24 sc (24 st).
Start stuffing the body.
Rnd 18: 5 sc, (1 dec, 2 sc) x 3, 7 sc (21 st).
Rnd 19: (4 sc, 1 dec, 1 sc) x 3 (18 st).
Rnd 20: (1 sc, 1 dec, 3 sc) x 3 (15 st).
Rnd 21: (3 sc, 1 dec) x 3 (12 st).
Finish stuffing the body. Do not stuff the tail.

Tail

The sequence of instructions consists of dividing the piece in two to crochet two fins (parts a and b).
Rnd 22a: 6 sc. Do not crochet the other st, but mark the following st on rnd 21.
Then start the next rnd by inserting the crochet hook in the 1st st made in rnd 22a. This leaves a hole that will be crocheted later (6 st).
Rnd 23a: 2 sc, 2 inc, 2 sc (8 st).
Rnd 24a: 3 sc, 2 inc, 3 sc (10 st).
To close the piece, make 1 sl st in the following st and ch 1. Insert the crochet hook in the st that follows the sl st and then in the st that precedes it, and make 1 sc. Make 3 more sc by crocheting the two thicknesses together, and ch 1 to finish.
Bring the yarn to the inside and cut it off flush with the surface.
Pull a white yarn through the st marked previously to crochet the 2nd part of the tail, keeping 6in (15cm) of starting yarn.
Ch 1.
Rnd 22b: 1 sc in the same st, 5 sc.
Start the following row by inserting the crochet hook in the 1st st made in rnd 22b (6 st).
Rnd 23b: 1 sc, 2 inc, 3 sc (8 st).
Rnd 24b: 3 sc, 2 inc, 3 sc (10 st).
Close this fin in the same way as the previous one.
Stop the starting yarn in the same way.
Sew the legs on each side of the body, 2 rnds behind the eyes and 2 st lower than the eyes.
Sew the two thicknesses simultaneously using 3 sewing stitches. Bring the yarn to the inside and then cut it off flush with the surface.
Embroider two whiskers on each side of the nose, straddling rnds 3 and 4.
If you wish, embroider or draw cheeks according to the instructions given in the *Basic Shapes* section, p. 30.

Crab

p. 20

Dimensions
Approximate length: 3 3/20in (8cm), including feet

Materials
› One 2.25mm crochet hook
› DMC Happy Cotton (¾oz–47yd [20g–43m]), shade 790, burnt orange, 7/20oz (10g); shade 762, white, 20in (50cm)
› Two 6mm (¼in) safety eyes

FEET x 6

In orange.
Ch 6, keeping 4in (10cm) of starting yarn. Starting in the 2nd st away from the crochet hook, make: 1 sl st, 1 sc, 1 inc, 1 sc; 1 sc and 1 sl st in the same st. Cut the yarn to a length of 4in (10cm). Tie the starting and ending yarns by making a double knot.

CLAWS x 2

In orange. Crochet in a spiral.
Rnd 1: 4 sc in a magic circle (4 st).
Rnd 2: (1 inc, 1 sc) x 2, small claw (ch 3, 2 sl st starting in the 2nd st away from the crochet hook). The small claw does not count in the st of the rnd (6 st).
Rnd 3: 1 inc, 5 sc (7 st).
Rnd 4: Make the 1st st by placing the small claw in front, to the outside of the large claw: 1 sc, 2 dec, 2 sc (5 st).
Stuff the start of the claw, then stop stuffing.
Rnds 5 and 6: 5 sc (5 st).
Cut the yarn to a length of 10in (25cm). Close the piece and keep the yarn for sewing.

BODY

1st part

In orange. Crochet in a spiral around the starting ch.
Rnd 1: Ch 5, 1 sc in the 2nd st away from the crochet hook; continuing along the ch: 2 sc; in the last st of the ch: 3 sc; coming back up the other side of the ch: 2 sc, 1 inc (10 st).
Rnd 2: 1 inc, 2 sc, 3 inc, 2 sc, 2 inc (16 st).
Rnd 3: 1 sc, 1 inc, 2 sc, (1 sc, 1 inc) x 3, 2 sc, (1 sc, 1 inc) x 2 (22 st).
Rnd 4: 1 inc, 4 sc, (1 inc, 2 sc) x 3, 2 sc, (1 inc, 2 sc) x 2 (28 st).
Rnd 5: 1 sl st, do not crochet the other st (28 st).
Mark the 26th st of rnd 4. Stop the yarn invisibly.

2nd part

In orange. Crochet in a spiral.
Rnds 1 to 4: Repeat the instructions of the 1st part.
Rnds 5 to 7: 28 st (28 st).
Insert the safety eyes between rnds 5 and 6, in st 17 and 23 of rnd 5. Using a needle and 6in (15cm) of white yarn, embroider a small line below and to the outside of each eye, quite close to the plastic eye. Tie the ends on the inside. Do the same with an orange yarn, but this time above and to the outside of each eye, as an eyebrow.
Position the 2 parts of the body back-to-back (back sides of work together). Crochet the next rnd by inserting the crochet hook in both parts at the same time, in the FLO, to have a thinner "seam" (the uncrocheted BL are thus invisible, on the inside of the body).
To avoid having to sew the legs on, add the 6 legs to the st indicated in rnd 8. To add a leg, first insert the crochet hook in the FL of the 2nd part of the body, then in the sl st that ends the leg (beside the knot), then in the FL of the 1st part of the body, and make 1 sl st. Legs 1, 2, and 6 must place the st toward the top. Legs 3, 4, and 5 must have the back side of the st toward the top. This way, all the

legs will curve inward toward the eyes.
Before making the last st, stuff the body.
Rnd 8: (1 sl st, 1 sl st adding 1 leg) x 2, 4 sl st, (1 sl st adding 1 leg, 1 sl st) x 3, 13 sc, 1 sl st, adding 1 leg (28 st).
Close invisibly, then bring the yarn inside the shell several times before cutting it off flush with the surface.
Sew the claws below and to the outside of the eyes, straddling rnd 7 of the 2nd part of the body.
Bring the yarns to the inside and cut them off flush with the surface.

Blue Tang

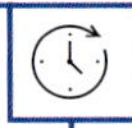 2 hours

p. 21

Dimensions
Approximate length: 2⅝in (6.5cm)

Materials
› One 2.25mm crochet hook
› DMC Happy Cotton (¾oz–47yd [20g–43m]), shade 798, royal blue, ¼oz (6g); shade 758, navy blue, 1/10oz (3g); shade 788, lemon yellow, 1/10oz (3g); shade 762, white, 20in (50cm)
› Two 6mm (¼in) safety eyes

LATERAL FINS x 2

In yellow.
In a magic circle, make: ch 2, 2 dc, ch 2, 1 sl st.
Cut the yarn to a length of 8in (20cm).

DORSAL FIN

In royal blue.
Ch 14, keeping 10in (25cm) of starting yarn.
Make 13 sl st, starting in the 2nd st away from the crochet hook. Cut the yarn to a length of 6in (15cm).

VENTRAL FIN

In royal blue.
Ch 10, keeping 10in (25cm) of starting yarn.
Make 9 sl st starting in the 2nd st away from the crochet hook. Cut the yarn to a length of 6in (15cm).

BODY

In royal blue. Crochet in a spiral. The royal blue yarn (RB) may be carried along as you make the color changes. The navy blue yarn (NB) and yellow yarn must be cut and tied in a knot on the back side of the work with each color change.
Rnd 1: 6 sc in a magic circle (6 st).
Rnd 2: 3 sc, 3 inc (9 st).
Rnd 3: 9 sc (9 st).
Rnd 4: 9 inc (18 st).
Rnd 5: 4 sc, 2 inc, 7 sc, 2 inc, 3 sc (22 st).
Rnd 6: 4 sc, (1 inc, 2 sc) x 2, 12 sc (24 st).
Rnd 7: 1 sc; NB: 2 sc; RB: 3 sc, 2 inc, 3 sc; NB: 2 sc; RB: 6 sc, 1 inc, 4 sc (27 st).
Rnd 8: 1 sc; NB: 2 sc; RB: 10 sc; NB: 2 sc; RB: 12 sc (27 st).
Rnd 9: 2 sc; NB: 2 sc; RB: 9 sc; NB: 2 sc; RB: 12 sc (27 st).
Rnd 10: 3 sc; NB: 2 sc; RB: 7 sc; NB: 2 sc; RB: 13 sc (27 st).

Insert the safety eyes between rnds 8 and 9, in st 3 and 15 of rnd 8. Using a needle and 6in (15cm) of white yarn, embroider a little line behind each eye, quite close to the plastic eye. Tie the ends on the inside. Start stuffing the front of the body.

Rnd 11: 4 sc; NB: 1 inc; RB: 7 sc; NB: 2 sc; RB: 1 sc in the same st, 8 sc, 1 inc, 4 sc (30 st).
Rnd 12: 2 sc; NB: 2 sc, 1 dec, 1 sc; RB: 6 sc; NB: 1 sc, 1 dec, 2 sc; RB: 6 sc, 1 dec, 4 sc (27 st).
Rnd 13: 1 sc; NB: 1 sc; RB: 2 sc; NB: 2 sc; RB: 6 sc; NB: 2 sc; RB: 2 sc; NB: 1 sc; RB: 10 sc (27 st).
Rnd 14: 1 sc; NB: 1 sc; RB: 2 sc; NB: 2 sc; RB: 1 sc; 1 dec, 3 sc; NB: 2 sc; RB: 2 sc; NB: 1 dec; RB: 7 sc, 1 dec (24 st).
Rnd 15: 1 sc; NB: 1 sc; RB: 2 sc; NB: 2 sc; RB: 1 sc, 2 dec, 1 sc; NB: 2 sc; RB: 2 sc; NB: 1 sc; RB: 2 sc, 2 dec, 1 sc (20 st).
Rnd 16: 2 sc; NB: 4 sc; RB: 2 dec; NB: 4 sc; RB: 2 sc, 2 dec (16 st).
Stuff the body.
Rnd 17: 2 sc; in yellow: 1 sc; NB: 1 sc, 1 dec; RB: 1 dec; NB: 1 dec, 1 sc; in yellow: 1 sc; RB: 2 sc, 1 dec (12 st).
Rnd 18: In yellow: 1 dec, 1 sc, 1 dec; RB: 1 sc; in yellow: (1 dec, 1 sc) x 2 (8 st).
Finish stuffing. Stop the RB and NB yarns.
Rnd 19: 1 inc, 1 sc, 3 inc, 1 sc, 2 inc (14 st).
Rnd 20: 2 sc, 1 inc, 6 sc, 1 inc, 3 sc, 1 sl st (16 st).
Cut the yarn to a length of 10in (25cm). Using a needle, close the body without stuffing the ventral fin. Insert the needle in the FLO, that is, those on the outside. Insert the needle in the next st (the 1st st of rnd 20) from the outside toward the inside, and then in the preceding st (the last sc of rnd 20), from the inside to the outside. Repeat this sewing stitch in the FLO 6 more times, and then bring the yarn to the inside and cut it off flush with the surface.
With the ending yarn, sew the lateral fins on each side of the body, 1 rnd behind the eyes and 1 st lower than the eye. Bring this yarn and the starting yarn to the inside, and cut it off flush with the surface.
Position the dorsal fin straddling rnds 8 to 17 of the body, along an imaginary line that would join the starting magic circle of the body to the top of the ventral fin. With the starting yarn, sew the lower loops of the ch. Then bring this yarn and the ending yarn to the inside, and cut them off flush with the surface.
Position the ventral fin the same way, straddling rnds 10 to 17 of the body.
Sew in the same way.